HOMER AND ME

by

Ressie Chrenshaw Watts

authorHOUSE™

1663 LIBERTY DRIVE, SUITE 200
BLOOMINGTON, INDIANA 47403
(800) 839-8640
WWW.AUTHORHOUSE.COM

First published by AuthorHouse 09/23/05

ISBN: 1-4208-7166-8 (sc)

Printed in the United States of America
Bloomington, Indiana

This book is printed on acid-free paper.

CHAPTER I

The New Place

The lead wagon in which we rode lurched up the narrow, gully-washed lane. We all strained to get a first glimpse of our new home through the low-hanging branches of maple and sweet gum trees that bordered the roadway on both sides. Papa, driving the team, said it would be a while yet, but all leaned forward anxiously, and I started to rise to my feet.

"Duck!" came Papa's warning - too late. I grabbed for Homer as a limb almost knocked me from the wagon. Blood ran down into my eye from a small cut above it, and a welt began to form on my cheek.

Mama, holding the twins in her lap, looked over her shoulder. "Oh, it's you! I thought Homer was hurt. Homer, you lay back. And you!" She glared at me. "You know better than to catch at a limb. Sit down. I'll tend to you later."

1

Homer squeezed my arm in sympathy. My throat was tight and choking but I knew that crying would get me nowhere. I shoved the pillow we had been sharing toward Homer.

"Here," I whispered. "She wants you to have it."

Blood and tears mingled to wash down my face. Homer looked pained, and he dabbed at the mess with his handkerchief and put his arm around me. We pulled the pillow close against us. It seemed that whatever happened to me was of little consequence to anyone but Homer. He was different. My bother loved me. From as far back as I could remember, he had been the one who cared about me and took my side in any problems that concerned us. Five years my senior, he had learned early in my life to "mind the baby," which I had been before the twins arrived. By now, in nearly six years together, the bond between us had grown steadily stronger. He was the only one who knew I could talk, which I could do as well as most. But I just found it far more rewarding to listen.

My mother never called me by my name; Ressie. Papa had named me and she suspected that the name was that of a woman in his past. Papa wouldn't explain and Mama resented me as well as the unknown lady.

Mama and the other members of the family believed there was something wrong with me. "It can't talk," she'd say, as though I wasn't a person. "Poor thing, how could she? She's . . . you know," and the finger would touch the forehead.

A midwife and nurse, Mama always spoke worriedly of me but never showed the least affection. At every opportunity she spoke of "Lung Sickness," glancing sideways at me. "It probably won't be with us long."

Skinny, frail and poorly, in Mama's terms, my birth had followed shortly after the death of a beautiful, plump and beloved child. I think Mama never forgave me for failing to replace her loss. Luckily, or disappointingly, I was never ill.

Homer, the younger son, was the only boy to follow five girls. Since there were plenty of girls among the thirteen children. I could understand Mama , favoring Homer. But it seemed to me and Homer, ever my protector, that Mama and the girls singled me out especially as the target of all their ill feelings.

Homer and I shared our dreams and plans. He even looked to me for counsel. I was happy to be accepted and respected by at least one person. Oftentimes I got us both into trouble with Mama. But Homer never laid blame on me.

Bumping along in the wagon, side by side, I dared not raise up again to see ahead, and at last with a jerk, the wagon pulled to a stop in front of our new home. All eyes turned to the wide veranda. A huge black man got up from an old chair and ambled down the steps and over to the wagon.

"How do, Mr. Crenshaw. We did all you said. Scrubbed the place and aired it out. Shore a big um'! There's fresh water settin' in the kitchen jus' like you said."

"Good, very good, Popper. This is Mis' Crenshaw," Papa motioned toward Mama. "Emma, this is Popper Paradise. He works for me at the sawmill. If you need help, let him know. And this is Blue, his son," Papa pointed to the boy who stood diggin his toes in the sand.

3

He was about Homer's age. "Blue, you take Homer and Ressie here and see they stay out of the way while we unload some of this," Papa continued, helping me from the wagon. He waved his hand toward the two loads behind us.

"You mean all, William. All! I want it all unloaded now," Mama was adamant. Papa helped her by taking the twins and handed one to Popper. "I can take care of myself, William. Take the babies to the porch. I'll make a pallet for them and her, (meaning me!), and Homer can watch over them. I'll see to things with the help of the other children." She jerked a quilt from a box behind the wagon seat and with an officious flounce strode over to the porch. Blue moved back as she pushed past me and said, "Don't let these babies fall off, and do stop your sniffling. You weren't hurt that bad, you know."

She settled the babies on the pallet and glowered at me. "If those babies fall, your backside will smart more then your face." I nodded wordlessly, and moved closer to the pallet. Turning to Blue, she said, "You, boy, fetch the water pail from the kitchen. Take Homer with you and mind, hurry it up. We are all thirsty."

Mama turned to the wagons and began to direct the unloading. I tucked a roll of the quilt under the pallet, making a barrier to help hold the babies. My face felt puffy and uncomfortable and I wished I could explore the big house as the other children were doing. Homer and Blue returned with the water and a gourd dipper. I gave the babies a drink and had one myself. They were as thirsty as I was.

Blue looked down at me for a moment then ran to the other end of the porch and returned with a clean rag. He shifted from one foot to the other and said politely, "If you all want, I kin fix your face so's it won't hurt."

I nodded and bent toward him, lifting my face.

"Fix it," Homer said to him and took over watching the babies for me.

Blue poured some of the water over the cloth and carefully washed my face. It was soothing. He then produced a vial of liquid from the deep recesses of his too-big overalls. Pouring a little on one corner of the cloth, he dabbed the cut over my eye. What it was, I never knew, but it worked. My face quit burning and the cut stopped bleeding. I sensed that Blue was somebody I could allow to hear me speak, but not yet. I smiled my appreciation.

"My Granny's cures always work, you all 'll see."

I touched the cut and finding it dry, I nodded and smiled again. Blue would be our friend. As the three wagons were unloaded, lights appeared throughout the house, but I still huddled in my appointed place beside the babies. They were fed and had fallen asleep while Mama's voice reverberated through the house. Men hurried in and out and my older sisters and brothers bore the brunt of Mama's tiredness and frustration.

Blue kept Homer and me entertained, telling wild scary tales about this house we were moving into.

"Ain't nobody lived here in this ole-haunted house since ol' Wilbur Morrison done hung hisself in that place under the back porch. So's you all better watch out. You all is gonna live right on an

5

old graveyard, almos'. It's just down the road a piece. But ifn you all come over to Granny's, I get her to give you a spook chaser charm. It work real good. Ain't no old ghos' ever do me no harm, cause I carry a good charm," He pulled a long bone out of the bottomless pocket and swung it round and round on a string, muttering something I couldn't understand. His last remark before he left us made me shiver with excitement.

"When you all hear them chains ratlin' you knows it's jus' ol' Morrison's ghos' draggin' them chains cause he were still wearin' them when they foun' him, hung fo' three days. He done run away from the gang!" With that, he ran to a gap in the paling fence and disappeared.

Homer and I were frightened. We huddled close, afraid to move until one of the older girls came to put the babies to bed and show us to our room. At last, too tired to appreciate any of it, I entered our new home. They brought milk and bread for our super. Straining my ears, not knowing whether the sounds I heard were Mama and Papa still moving about below or the ghostly chains being dragged across the floor.

When I finally got to explore it, I found the house enormous. Large rooms, wide porches and a big cavern under the long back porch that was used for storage. Rain or shine, Homer and I played on the high back steps or under the porch where we searched for signs of Mr. Morrison's blood in the soft earth and poked about looking for odd links of his chain. When it was necessary for me to play alone, I poured out my heart to my rag doll Dimples, a stuffed printed form made from a 50-pound sack of Dolly Dimples flour.

Talking to imaginary people who loved me became a way of life. Each of them spoke kindly, and like Homer, never, never, made fun of me.

I was kept safe from "catching anything" in the secluded back yard, enclosed with a paling fence that Papa made, head high and pig tight. The Sunday trip to church and an occasional visit to relatives or a close neighbor were the rare excursions in my life.

It came September. From the top of the steps where I could look across the wide expanse of the farm, my world was a panorama of beautiful colors. Misty dawns hesitated for a moment before brightening into day. Sunsets lingered in purple and brilliant gold as if for a last goodnight kiss. It was a lovely autumn.

One morning Papa brought a newspaper home and showed the headlines to the family. He said the story reported that the Democrat Wilson just might be voted in to replace the Republican Taft. I always listened to Papa. He seemed to know everything and I could tell that the newspaper's information worried him. It did not interest me at all. However, there was news that did. Important news!

After morning prayers, Mama looked directly at me and announced to all the family, "You're six years old today and that means you will be going to school, just like any other child your age." In her view, of course, I was not like any other child. She sat back in her chair looking at me in her peculiar way. It was as though she was thinking that when I got to school the whole world would find out what a trial I was to her. "Then we'll see about you," she added.

Papa peered over his glasses, "Emma, enough."

"Humph," Mama said and began to assign jobs for the day.

At first, the school idea was a shock. But what a delightful one!

"Now you will get a tablet and pencil," Homer said, happy for me.

My fingers itched for them. And I was to have a book of my own! These precious supplies were to be bought from old man Payne, the peddler. He traveled over the country trading. He also tried to gyp most of his customers out of hot meals. He was fat, baldheaded, squinty-eyed and smelled to high heaven. But for us country children, he was the bearer of treasures galore.

Homer and I watched eagerly for his covered "store on wheels." From the top steps we saw the wagon, far down the road, and it wasn't long before we smelled it too. He had taken some chickens in trade and a few had died from thirst. A weary pig half walked and dragged behind the wagon on a rope. It squealed in protest, and a yearling calf, similarly towed, bawled continuously.

Homer called Mama and she quickly gathered her list of things needed. Being a Christian, she was furious at Mr. Payne's treatment of dumb animals, "gloriously angry" was the way she put it, and she stood waiting for him to approach within earshot.

"Mr. Payne!" Her voice rang with authority, "You will please to put that poor pig and calf in yonder pen and feed and water them. And give those poor chickens a drink too. I have need of some of your supplies and will deduct a proper amount for the cost of the feed, if you please!"

There wasn't much he could do if he wanted to sell Mama anything, so he pulled the weary calf and pig into the pen. They were too tired and relieved to do more than drink their fill and lie down. Homer and I brought fresh water to the chickens in the wire coop under his wagon where they'd suffered from the dust brought up from the wagon wheels. Mr. Payne removed the dead ones to a cardboard box.

When the animals were taken care of to Mama's satisfaction, Mr. Payne opened his well - stocked wagon. Whatever he didn't do properly, he did keep a neat wagon. There were bolts of cloth, lace, ribbons, buttons, needles, yarn, patterns, scissors and thread, all guarded by hinged boards to hold them in place. The other side was my favorite; pens, ink, pencils, tablets, slates, slate pencils and books someone had used and wanted to pass along. In the middle of the wagon, a tray with a hinged top held pots, pans, lids, fly swatters, hammers, nails, tacks, shoe leather and oddments.

Mama pointed her finger at me, "This one starts school. She needs a slate, a pencil and a tablet, and we also need a Third Book if you have one." She dug through the contents of a wooden box, glaring at Mr. Payne as she pawed, and wrinkling her nose in distaste at the odor.

Mr. Payne rubbed his belly with one hand and lifted his greasy felt hat with the other, scratching his bald pate with his little finger.

"Now Mrs. Crenshaw, you know I got jus' about everything you need, and my price will be in your favor if you feel you can spare a bit of food for me. I ain't et all day, and the missus is ailing so's I reckon she won't be fixing me nothin' iffen I do get home."

9

"We'll see, we'll see," answered Mama.

She was as shrewd as he when it came to making a deal. She laid out bolts of cloth and notions; pencils and paper for each child who would be attending school. Last, she came up with a Third Book for Homer.

After all the dickering, Mama finally gave in and invited Mr. Payne to stay for supper. Homer and I had to pump water for his mules and feed the pig and calf. Neighbors said that he was mean not only to his animals but to his wife also, and I thought about her as I watered the cooped chickens again. I wondered what kind of a person she was. Maybe I would be able to find out, now that I was going to school.

CHAPTER II

School Time

Attending school was an eye-opener for me. First; our back gate, formerly a bar to the world outside, was unlatched, and I went in and out just like people. I looked at Homer and smiled and went in and out several times, just to have the satisfaction of doing so. Homer stood waiting patiently for me, understanding fully. Pokey stood resolutely inside the fence, wagging his tail, happy for me, Mama was the only one not pleased.

"Stop dwadling," she said and took me by the hand.

I resisted, I wanted to go to school but not in what I was wearing. My dress was a hand-me-down checkered print with a red bow which I thought was hideous. Furthermore, my drawers were a little too big. They slipped down and threatened to come off every time I moved. I began to cry.

11

Mama was never one to listen to argument. She dragged me away from the gate and down the road. She pulled me by one hand all the way to school. With my other hand, I wiped my eyes or nose or held up my drawers, depending on which was the most urgent need.

At school my teacher was Miss Harris. I could tell that she and I were not going to get along very well from the moment Mama led me into the school room. Mama performed introductions. "This is Ressie," she said.

I stared up at Miss Harris. I said nothing.

"She can talk," Mama assured. "I've heard her. She's just stubborn and won't. It's your job to teach her, and you can just make her learn."

Silent, I found a place and sat down.

In spite of that unpromising beginning, school thrilled me. I loved the whole idea, reading, writing, even arithmetic. The smells were especially dear to me; new paper, ink, chalk, books and cedar pencils. I was forever smelling of the paper, pressing my nose in my book.

"She ain't right," whispered a girl behind me.

"Yeah," was the reply. "Not all there."

Over and over I heard remarks like these. I didn't care a whit. Though it all, I maintained my silence.

My First Book, "Elson's First Reader", sent shivers of pure delight through me. The first lesson was short:

Bow wow wow. Whose dog art thou?

Little Tommy Tinker's dog. Bow wow wow!

I'd read it to myself many times, but in view of my, "disability", I had not been called upon to read in class.

One day I listened to the stammering utterances of several of the pupils. The teacher read the lesson over then called on me, without much enthusiasm.

"Will you please read for us?" she said, nodding at me.

Mute, I sat staring at her.

Miss Harris repeated her question with strained politeness. "Will you please read for us, Ressie?"

She had used the magic word. At the unexpected sound of my given name, I stood up, tall and straight. I read the lesson, another silly poem, with the proper enunciation and elocution, then politely asked if I might read further.

Miss Harris was too dumbfounded to do more than nod. The class sat as if petrified. I read on and on until I wasn't sure of the next page and primly sat down. Miss Harris dropped into her chair in a lump and glared at me. I felt sure she would have slapped me down had she dared.

I smiled at her and refused to say another word. She knew why, too. She had just told the other teacher in my presence that I was the stupidest person she had ever had in her class. She had thought me too dumb to understand.

On the way home, I told Homer what I had done. He grinned and whooped me on the back.

Miss Harris made a point of coming to our house the next evening and reported how well she had overcome my "problem and fears," as she put it. She preened herself on how well I could read and assured Mama and Papa that I was really a smart child, though my inability to speak did make it difficult for her to teach me.

I was in the room, overhearing. "Miss Harris told Miss Cate I was the stupidest kid she ever saw!" I said boldly, in the midst of her gushing praise of herself.

Miss Harris merely looked startled, but Mama, gathering her most ferocious expression, turned on me. "Go to the back yard I'll attend to you directly," she said sternly.

I went.

When Mama came to punish me for my out burst, Papa followed along and laid a restraining hand on her arm. "Leave the child be, Emma," he said. "I believe her."

"You'll live to regret this, William!" Mama retorted.

She was furious, but I added a name to my list of heroes; Homer, and now Papa.

Miss Harris or not, school was for me a real and sought-after pleasure. I was quick to learn. Pen and paper became my companions. Written lessons were a snap. I topped anyone in the class except in arithmetic. I hated that subject. Being better in class only added to my unpopularity. I didn't mind too much, though I would have appreciated a girl friend in whom I could confide.

Although my brother was older than I, we always seemed to be in the same room. Homer was a problem to the teacher in a different way than I was. He livened up one dull, hot afternoon by dipping Eula Sutton's hair into the green ink on the desk behind her.

For recitation, the class sat on two slatted benches up in front of the teacher. My brother usually managed to sit on the rear bench, and one day he tied Beulah Young's braids around the slat in front of him. When she tried to jump up to answer a question, as was her fashion, she was jerked back onto the bench with a snap. For that prank, Homer stood with his nose in a ring the teacher chalked on the blackboard, and I seethed with anger.

We would have our revenge.

In that part of Arkansas where we lived, most people let their pigs run loose during the day and called them to come in at night. Along in the evening, we could sit on our back steps and hear a chorus of, "So-o-o! So-o-o! Here pig."

A few days after the blackboard incident, as Homer and I were on our way to school, we came by a rail fence, and there, bedded down in the angle of the rails was a spotted sow with her five baby pigs.

"That's Steele's old sow," said Homer and looked at me out of the corner of his eye.

"Sure is," I agreed. I knew what he was thinking. Homer took a fruit tart from his lunch pail and broke off a piece. "So-o. So-o," he called and dropped a piece of fruit tart in the path.

The sow lumbered to her feet and came over to investigate. She looked huge when she stood up, her back almost level with my shoulders. She gobbled up the first piece of fruit tart, and Homer broke off another for her. "So-o" he called, moving on down the path.

With pieces of sandwich and fruit tart and a boiled egg, we got the sow and her baby pigs to follow us along the path to the schoolyard. Once there, we ran into the class room as if the sow had nothing to do with us, and waited for the results that were certain to come when the sow discovered where the school lunches were kept.

All of us kids brought a lunch to school, in a pail, an oat box, or a folded newspaper, if there was nothing else. During the morning, the lunches sat lined up in a hall which was open at both ends for ventilation. There was nothing to keep the sow from getting at them, and she did.

Shortly after the first group of pupils was called up front to recite, we began hearing noises from outside the classroom. Newspaper rustled, and the round lid of a lunch pail clattered as it rolled down the step. Finally, an unmistakable grunt got Miss Harris' attention. "I do believe there is something in the hall," she said, and went to see what it was.

Miss Harris was not exactly used to pigs, and the sight of one rooting through the lunches in the hall set her back some. "Ge' away from there!" she cried.

The sow was too busy eating a baked sweet potato to pay any attention. Homer and I hugged ourselves. Several of the girls giggled. Miss Harris appealed for aid.

"You older boys, come and chase this pig away."

Lessons were forgotten. Everyone in the class rushed out, some to protect their lunches and others just to have a better look at what was going on. The noise brought Miss Carson's class out of their room on the other side of the hall.

In the confusion, the little pigs took off running, and some of the kids chased after them, They dodged all over the school yard and wound up back at the lunches where they started. Homer jumped on the sow's back and rode her through the hall at a trot to add to the excitement, but he scrambled off before she had time to get aggravated at him.

Miss Harris was just helpless. It took Miss Carson to cope with the situation. She went back into her classroom for a broom and gave the a sow a good whack with the sweeping end. The sow let herself be herded out of the schoolyard. She knew she was not supposed to be there as well as anybody did.

With in a week or so, some men came and built a shelf in the hall. We were told to put our lunches on that so they would be safe from any animals which happened along. Lunchtime went back to being more predictable after that.

For Homer and me, lunch meant a large fried fruit tart, a boiled egg, two sandwiches of jelly or cold meat and always fresh fruit of some kind. We did not take milk, but often took cider to school. Many of the pupils ate as well as we did, but the poorer ones had only cold baked sweet potatoes and cornbread.

One day, we devised a remedy for this inequality. Homer told the teacher that Mama had given us castor oil the night before. Many times during the morning, with painful grimaces, we would clutch our abdomens and ask to be excused. Each time that we left the room, we took from our own bucket or the pail of a well-fed classmate and added food to the scantier lunches. At noontime, pleasure and dismay were clearly written on many of the faces around us. Homer and I glowed with good feeling at what we had accomplished.

When something impressed Homer and me as being unjust, we could usually think up a plan to make it balance out, at least to our satisfaction. We did not mind working hard to accomplish our goal, and the risk of being caught in our preparations only added to the thrill when we were successful. Once in a while, we succeeded better than we planned. I know we did in the case of Maybelle Hoglin.

There were about sixteen houses in the three-mile stretch of Sawmill Road along which Homer and I walked to school, and classmates of ours lived in almost every one. Some of the houses were accessible only by gully washed lanes, and the main road twisted and turned around natural obstacles until the three miles often times seemed more like ten, but to all the school children, the walk offered a place for socializing and play.

The youngest in the group played tag or a form of hopscotch. Some had a jump rope cut from an old lead rope for a horse or cow, a prized possession. Skipping rope made the walk to school pass quickly, providing a hapless friend could be persuaded to carry someone else's books and lunch pail. The older boys and girls cast adoring eyes at which ever one of the opposite sex was in favor at the moment. For all, the walk was an enjoyable event.

By the time the school was in sight and the last boy or girl had joined the group, we make a sizable crowd, but no matter how many were present, attention always seemed to center on Maybelle Hoglin. This probably struck her as being only natural, since she thought she was better and more attractive than anyone else. She was slender but well rounded and had wavy blond hair. When she cared to, she presented merry laughter and twinkling blue eyes, which the older boys found very much to their liking. Most of them performed unusual feats of skill and daring to get her attention, climbing trees, walking the rail fence, catching a partridge with bare hands or killing a snake. Any problem which might arise was an opportunity to impress Maybelle.

On our way to school, there was a shortcut that led down through the woods and across Chilton Creek. The creek was deep in some places and shallow in others. We crossed it on a fallen log where the water was about waist deep in normal weather, though it would reach dangerous stages after a heavy rain. Even then, the log was wide enough and strong enough for safety.

All the children in our group could cross easily, but every day we had to wait for Maybelle to clutch her breast and gasp, "Oh, I'm so afraid." Finally, showing favor to two of her many admirers, she would timidly ask, "Please, Cliff, or Bert, will you please help me?"

The trip across the log would have been far less dangerous for her alone, but that was not the object. With a little hand-holding and shy looks from willing males, she would land on the far bank with a sigh and a quick hug to express her gratitude. In this devious way, physical contact was made which, in turn made the chosen boys slaves of Maybelle until the day she called on another boy to help her. Chagrin showed plainly on the face of the boy in disfavor, and Maybelle would toss her curls and sling tart remarks at the one she was "teaching who's boss."

One day Maybelle decided to take Homer as her favorite. When he was not so easily persuaded as she thought he would be, she said cattily, "Oh, you better hold onto that skinny sister of yours. She might fall in and an ol' water moccasin would swallow her right down. She wouldn't even show in that ol' snake."

"You can cross by yourself, or fall in," replied Homer. "I don't care which. You jus' better keep your mouth shut, Maybelle Hoglin. You think you're so much. Jus' cause you got to have your way all the time. Better watch out, Miss Smart Alec."

Homer was still a little young for Maybelle, and he resented any remark made about me. I could tell when he looked at me that he was already alive with a plan to get even.

Saturday afternoon, Homer and I armed ourselves with a saw and a tow sack and set out for Chilton Creek. The water under the crossing log was about normal depth, which made our task a little awkward but not too dangerous.

Homer tied the tow sack to the log with the calf rope so I could stand in the sack and help with the work. About half way out, he found a spot in the log free of knots and limbs and began to saw the log under water. I gathered the debris that came loose and dropped it into the sack. At first there was bark and a few vines, but eventually he was sawing away at solid timber. It was hard work, and I offered words of encouragement. We did not have to talk of what we were doing. Every time we looked at each other, we laughed until tears streamed down our faces as we visualized Maybelle at a dripping disadvantage.

When there was just the upper edge of the log left, Homer and I took long limbs and pushed and beat the remains of sawed, wet wood into the main stream. We had saved some green moss and bark, we placed this around the tree until it looked normal. Then, Homer pulled me to shore, and with our tow sack full of telltale log scraps, we were on our way home.

Homer dumped the evidence in a stump hole in the pasture. I spread the sack on top of the calf pen to dry, and he replaced the rope.

We waited, Sunday evening it rained. In Sunday school I had prayed for rain, so I knew God approved what we had done, I relaxed.

On Monday morning, we joined the boys and girls with reports of what we had done or had to do over the weekend. The chores were familiar to all; picked up rocks all day Saturday, cleaned the yard, shelled corn. Very few had had any kind of fun things to do. Maybelle told us how well her solo had been received in church. I thought she was telling the wrong audience, since we all went to church and had heard her violin solo ourselves. It sounded like a mouse with his tail in a trap, squeaky and without tone quality.

Finally, we approached Chilton Creek, but when Homer and I saw what Sunday's rain had done, we suddenly lost our enthusiasm for the trick we were playing on Maybelle. Deep swift water was rushing just under the log where we usually crossed. The lowest part of the log looked wet and slick, dangerous even if we had not sawed it from underneath. I glanced at Homer uncertainly, wondering what would happen if Maybelle could not swim. He was scared too.

"Better let me go first,"he blurted.

All eyes turned on him as if he might have lost his sanity. Everybody knew Maybelle went first.

She went first again, though in view of the high water, she permitted Cliff to walk behind her holding on to her waist. He carried both her books and pails on his back, fastened with a strap. Maybelle giggled and put one hand on his, reaching out in front with the other, as if scared.

Perhaps, had Maybelle gone alone, all would have been well with her, but just at the proper place, she glanced coyly over her shoulder and pretended to lose her balance. As she twisted back to clutch at Cliff's hand, the log gave way, and both Cliff and Maybelle were floundering in the swirling water.

It was not like what Homer and I had visualized on Saturday afternoon. Kids were yelling. Maybelle was really scared. Homer grabbed my jump rope and the Sutton girl's and tied them together. Holding to a limb of the broken log, he got close enough to Cliff to toss him one end of the rope, and Cliff caught Maybelle just as she was going under.

The boys on shore pulled and tugged until the victims were safe on the bank. Two of the girls took off their raincoats and wrapped Maybelle in them. It was closer to school than home, so the group gathered lunch pails and books and went on by the main road with many "what-if's."

Homer handed my jump rope to me with a grin and said, "Don't worry. It'll dry."

"Can't hurt that ol' thing," I replied.

He knew I was not referring to the rope.

Maybelle's father, together with Papa and several neighbors, felled four huge trees and nailed them together, forming a path bridge to school. It bridged more than a rushing stream. Maybelle had to plan new ways to attract attention after that.

Everything taken together, school rapidly broadened my world. I learned a lot from watching my classmates. And official lessons expanded my horizon farther still. The "Second" and "Third" Readers opened a whole new concept of living for me. They were full of wonderful stories which I delighted in reading to my brother and Pokey. When I read, I was transported back in time, experiencing every exciting event.

The stories were a ritual for us. Adventure stories like "Ali Baba and The Forty Thieves" had to be read under the house for the right atmosphere. "The King of The Golden River" seemed out of place everywhere except the top of the back porch steps where Homer and I could glimpse the river through the tangled scope of oak trees. Each story required a special place.

I had grown quickly, once started, and no longer had much trouble keeping up with my brother in the antics of childhood. I could walk a rail fence without falling, "Skin-a-Cat" on the rafters in the barn or a low-hanging branch, and swing out over the river, clinging to a wild grape vine. All this led to some well-developed muscles.

My life, however, was not all school and play.

CHAPTER III

All Work - - No Play

Everyone at our house was required to work at whatever job he was capable of doing. I have often thought Mama should have been a general, The way she managed everybody and everything. After breakfast she mapped out the day's work, and woe to the one who did not follow her instructions. When Mama decided I was old enough and big enough, she assigned me two daily jobs; feeding the chickens and bringing in wood for the huge black cook stove.

The baby chicks grew to depend on me. They would jump into my lap and peck at my face. They loved me, or I imagined they did. I found names for them and could distinguish one from another. I hated to see them grow into fryers, setting hens and roosters, but I learned early that nothing ever, not ever, stays the same for very long.

The baby chicks were a pleasure. Not so, my other chore. I had nothing personal against the cook stove. In fact, I had a special reason to be grateful to it. I had not forgotten how it kept me warm when I was a baby. But the endless task of bringing in wood for my second mother soon wore my gratitude thin.

Before I grew old enough for the job, anyone climbing the back stairs to the porch carried up an armload of the wood which had been previously stacked under the edge of the house. Now, it was up to me to fetch all the wood the stove consumed, and our cook stove was the hungriest thing I ever saw. I named her Mrs. Blackie, and she became my "Trial and Tribulation," a phrase I had often heard Mama use in referring to me.

After school in winter, dark came early. It took armload after armload to fill the wood-box, and I was sometimes afraid to go out in the dark. Each time I passed Mrs. Blackie, she crackled with decisive laughter at my fear, then gobbled the wood I brought with a sputtering sound.

Early next morning the stove was ravenous again, and by evening she had contrived to empty the wood-box for me. When I went into the kitchen after school for a snack, she would grimace coldly at me. "Hurry, child, hurry. I'm hungry too, you know."

The cook stove had little windows in front with a slide shutter. When they were open, Mrs. Blackie was always laughing at me. Many times I have excused myself from the kitchen table and closed the mouth of that grinning, black iron ape with a slam of the shutter. It made my family laugh, but I found that preferable to the laughter of the stove.

On Sundays and holidays, Mrs. Blackie gobbled wood with gleeful delight until she was glowing hot. Then, she simmered in utter contentment, her belly-oven full of perfectly cooked food. After the food was consumed, she smirked and purred as the tea kettle and reservoir steamed with hot water.

Mama was proud of that stove. She rubbed her down with a blackening carefully concocted from tallow, soot and a bit of soap. Mrs. Blackie would wink at me as Mama finished.

If I shirked, which to my credit was not often, Papa would go out before breakfast and bring in the wood. He never scolded me, never accused, but I ate cold leftovers for breakfast. The rest of the family began the day with hot biscuits, meat, eggs, jam, honey, molasses and hominy. With that contrast on each side of me at the table, a plate of cold hominy and strap molasses was enough to keep me industrious.

Mama seemed to delight in piling work on me, gradually, she added to my jobs until very little time was left for play. Homer and I made a game of our work whenever we could. We enjoyed every moment when we worked together.

Some of our jobs were seasonal. In the fall, Homer and I accompanied Mama to the woods. There, under her direction, we gathered the wild plants basic to home remedies: butterfly root, black-haw bark and berries, ginseng root, rattlesnake weed root, witch hazel bark, wild cherry bark and sassafras root. My brother would dig where Mama said, while I gathered the herbs and put them in baskets. Back home again, Mama washed and dried all these wonders and stored them for future use.

She prepared herbs for seasoning in the same meticulous way, but the medicinal ones had a special importance, not only for us. Mama acted as nurse and doctor to many of the people around the country, both white and black. She knew how to make healing brews and salves from all the plants we gathered, and by spring her supply of them was almost always gone.

Apple time meant other seasonal jobs for my brother and me. Our whole family joined together in making apple cider and later fought the yellow jackets for the privilege of drinking it. Homer and I helped pick the apples and load them into the wagon which my older brother hauled with a team to the cider press beside the smokehouse. The apples were then crushed with mauls in a large trough. They were forced into one end where a wedge was placed against the board and tightened. The juice ran in a steady stream from a hole in one end of the trough. Homer and I drank the delicious juice until we sloshed when we jumped up and down. Mama canned the juice the family did not drink and put two huge barrels by for vinegar.

Apples also had to be dried. Two trees were selected for this process, sweet apples of the late-summer ripening. These had to be gathered carefully by hand to avoid bruising, and we carried them, a basketful at a time, to the shady back veranda where the whole family, except Papa and the older boys, joined in paring and slicing them for drying.

It was a happy time. Homer and I sang with the others and listened rapturously to often-told stories. Wonderful indeed was a visit from someone whose stories we had not heard. Tales followed one another while the apples were cored and sliced quite thin. The proper cutting was an art.

Last, the apples were strung on a thin rope, ready to lay on old sheets on top of the tin roofed barn to dry. This was a job for my brother and me. We were told to lay the strings of slices singly and close together. The temperature was ninety, and the tin roof was hot enough to make us dance. We came off the roof almost ready to collapse and were allowed to do nothing until the next "laying" was ready, in order to recuperate. We made a beeline to the fig tree where the dust was thick and cool and relieved our burning feet. Squawking in displeasure, chickens scattered from their dust baths at our approach.

We always looked for spiders under the fig tree and killed them if we could. Killing a spider was supposed to make it rain, and a good rain would mean no more climbing on the hot barn roof for a day at least. Even when the rain failed to come, Homer and I still felt satisfied if we had killed three or four spiders. We knew we had done what we could to bring our apple drying job to a quicker end.

Mama added several large white meal sacks of dried apples to the store of smoke house treasures before she was satisfied. She stored a like amount of other dried fruits there: peaches, apricots and pumpkin.

Nothing went to waste from the apples. Even the peels were dried. Mama used them to make cider. Into an oak keg she put successive layers of dried apple peeling, ripe persimmons and molasses until the keg was packed half to three-quarters full. Several pails of soft water were poured over this mixture and left to stand.

After a time, the cider was drained off and put into another keg which had a spigot. Homer and I were allowed to have a taste. We thought it was very good.

Although Papa's sawmill kept him very busy, even he found time to make peach and apricot brandy, grape and scuppernong wine, and malt beer. These were kept for special occasions and sickness. Anybody could feel well or sleep soundly if they drank enough of Papa's brew.

Mama put up jars and jars of preserves; pear, peach, grape, strawberry, dewberry, blackberry and huckleberry. I know there were a lot. I washed the jars and cleaned out the white lumps of spider eggs that accumulated from one year to the next. Mama inspected my work, and if she found any dirt, back came the jar for a second washing.

By fall, our cellar was packed. Besides the preserves, it hoarded apples wrapped in papers and packed in gum-wood barrels, brine dills, huge crocks of sauerkraut, winter potatoes and dry onions. On the floor of the cellar in an elevated spot sat churns of curd, crocks of home-churned butter, jars of thick buttermilk and churnings of fresh sweet milk, set to sour. A hogshead of thick sorghum cane molasses was turned on its side with a spigot at the best height for dispensing. A basket of fresh eggs hung from one of the cellar beams.

Homer and I were called on to make frequent trips to the cellar, and we cordially detested going. Snakes were drawn to the even temperature and the abundant supply of mice, and we were both petrified of snakes. My brother and I were always sent to the cellar together, and we never loitered, no matter what chores waited for us upstairs. I could imagine a snake lurking behind every barrel.

Filling the cellar for winter required a large summertime garden, and Homer and I had our share of weeding and watering it. There were muskmelon, watermelon, sweet potatoes, peanuts, corn, eggplant, kale, okra, sorghum-cane and more.

Mama also planted a small patch of cotton. Homer and I hated that cotton patch. Horned worms invaded it periodically, and their sting was terrible. I was deathly afraid of the awful things. They were worse than the cellar. The older girls helped Mama card cotton from that patch for quilts, but I think the real reason she planted it was to keep all us children out of mischief. If there was one thing Mama did not tolerate, it was idle hands.

Mama, and the family cow, Snowball, eventually added another chore to my list in the shape of a baby calf. Snowball was a good milker of undetermined breeding, white with several golden brown spots. A growth probably inherited from some ancient ancestor formed a large white ball between her horns and provided the inspiration for her name. When Papa brought her home as a gift from one of Mama's patients in return for some nursing, the cow was immediately christened snowball. Having a calf gave her distinction. She was known ever after as Mrs. Snowball. I would have been happy if she had gone without her distinction.

Until the calf was six weeks old, I had to watch and see that he got only two teats of the cow while nursing. The other two were reserved for the family milk supply. Guarding the family's teats was a sloppy, miserable job from which I emerged exhausted and covered

31

with calf slobber. My feet itched from the cow manure. I hated the job though I loved the calf. I named him Slowbo. He would take his own sweet time drinking, and when he finally finished, I had to push, pull and coax him into a nearby calf pen. Afterward, my first stop was always the spring house where I tried to wash the sweet calf smell from my body.

It was not too soon for me when Papa decided it was time to take the calf away from his mother. "Let Ressie and Homer take it to the edge of the melon patch near that old cemetery, Emma," he told Mama. "The grass is coming on tender there, and the calf will keep them occupied."

Next morning Mama gave us last minute instructions, and we were eager to be on our way. We took cookies and sandwiches wrapped in a checkered napkin for our lunch. There was water to be had from a spring near the old cemetery.

Blue joined us when his chores were done.

While the calf dozed in a shady spot, we three lay in the tall grass playing, "You want to do this." Each one in turn would think of some preposterous thing and ask the others if they wanted to do it. They had to say yes, or no, before the task was put into words. The results were often funny, great sport and high adventure.

"You want to do this?" I asked.

"Yes," said Blue.

Homer shook his head.

I grinned. "Set on bird's backs and fly across the field."

"Shucks," said Homer. "I wish I'd said that."

Sometimes we made rather nasty suggestions.

"You want to do this?" asked Blue.

"Maybe," I said cautiously, not sure if I should trust the glint in his eye.

"Eat a horse's turd."

"Yuk!" exclaimed Homer and I simultaneously. Then we rolled in the grass and laughed and thought of other outlandish things, each trying to top the one before.

"You two really want to do this?" asked Homer solemnly.

"Sure we do," I said. I sensed a new adventure from the tone of his voice.

"You betcha," agreed Blue, eager to get in on the fun, whatever it was.

"Tomorrow when we bring the calf out, we'll dig up a dead person in this ol' cemetery;"

"Gord!" Blue said, a little shook.

I thought a moment after having said yes. I couldn't back out, but I had to have a valid reason for going on, at least in my own mind. A sudden inspiration came to me.

The preacher said at old man Green's funeral, "Let his spirit go," or something like that. We could open up one of the graves and let the spirit go free. That'd be okay.

Blue shook his head. "I'll pay my fine. What you all want? I ain't about to fool 'round wit' no dead person. Specially no white dead person. No siree!"

Seeing a way out of a little work, Homer said promptly, "Help me stack wood. Two times and you're square."

33

"Deal," Blue answered him quickly. It was no real hardship. He probably would have helped anyway.

After our evening chores, we secretly hid a pick and shovel in a convenient place. We picked them up next day as we led the calf out.

Blue didn't show up at all.

The day was hot and sultry. Thunder heads formed in the west. Bees and bugs buzzed listlessly, hanging in midair.

Homer and I were unfamiliar with the proper burial position, but he decided to dig near a fallen and decayed wooden marker, first on one side, then on the other, until we were successful. He set to work. It was rather easy at first, though the ground had packed and quite a few pine saplings covered the area.

It got hotter. Sweat poured off Homer's face. He wiped his forehead with the sleeve of his shirt. Leaving a dirty streak, which Mama was sure to notice. I got him a drink from the nearby spring, and he sat down to rest, puffing and sipping the cool water.

The earth began to smell sour, and the adventure lost some of its attraction for me. Homer let me spade for a few minutes. I felt a little sick, but I knew I would lose face if I acted too much like a girl, so I kept digging. "Sure wish we could let that spirit out of here soon," I said. "I'm gittin' doggone tired."

Homer took the pick and began with renewed energy. "He's out!" he shouted suddenly, holding up a bone, green and coated with particles of soil.

I looked and gulped. "He sure is. Now, let's cover the hole."

"Wait! Wait a minute." Homer picked up an object and we ran to the spring to wash it off. It was a buckle or a brooch and had a real ruby for the main stone, surrounded by small diamonds. Some of the smaller stones were missing, but I thought it was still a beautiful piece of jewelry.

"Here," said Homer, "you can hold it awhile. That's all anyone can do with that stuff anyway. Hold it and look at it. I'll fill up the hole."

When he had filled in the grave, I placed the piece of jewelry carefully in a small hole in one of the pine trees. We set the rotted headboard upright and lay in the tall grass to talk of our secret. We were brought out of the reverie by lightning and thunder. The atmosphere was a dull yellow-green. Wind had started up, and huge raindrops began to fall.

We gathered our tools, untied the calf and headed for the house on the run.

"The spirits are mad at us." I gasped. "Just like Blue said they'd be."

"No, they ain't!" Homer was exuberant. "We let that poor ol' spirit out, and he's jus' having hisself a time."

By the time we got back, Blue had put my chicks in the coop and was helping get the baby ducks into the shed.

"See? What'd I tell you," he whispered. "You all shore 'nuff done it. We be lucky ol' tornado don' take us right off this earth."

The weather took over, slamming, blowing and whirling. It tore the sheet metal roof straight off the barn. We crouched in the cellar, sure that our messing around with the dead was the cause of the untimely storm. In reality that storm did us a big favor. The creek flooded and washed away the evidence of what we had done. Our secret was safe.

Blue told us many wild and weird tales of the results of "foolin' with the dead," enough to erase any desire to release other spirits. They would just have to remain imprisoned for the rest of time before the resurrection.

It was several days before we took the calf out again. We decided to tie him at the edge of the melon patch in the shade of an old peach tree. There were several rotted stumps nearby, and I fastened the rope around one while Homer and Blue found some melons to cool in the spring for use later.

The calf became restless, and I went to check. I saw the trouble immediately. The rope had rubbed the bark away from a hornets nest, and they quickly covered both the calf and me. I slipped the rope off the stump and the frightened calf ran, dragging me behind him while the hornets buzzed furiously, following us. They stung the calf and me many times before they were satisfied.

"Turn him loose," yelled Homer and Blue. "Turn loose of the calf, Ressie!"

I would have been glad to if I could, but the loop in the rope had tightened around my wrist, and I had to keep up or be dragged bodily. My steps were literally giant size.

Mama and the girls had been stuffing mattresses when they heard the yelling, and they ran to the top step to be able to see what was going on. My predicament was sure funny to them. They laughed and laughed.

Not me. By the time the hornets were finished, my face and head were an unholy sight, swollen and grotesque. Mama put soda paste on the stings and bathed my wounds in vinegar. I was sick for several days.

My brother and Blue brought me flowers and snail shells and carried the baby chicks in for me to hold. Blue said he had done a spell that would make me get well quickly, and it must have worked. In a week I was almost back to normal size with only a few black and blue patches here and there.

While the swelling lasted my sisters found my looks very funny. "She's fat now!" they teased.

Homer was furious with them. "Don't worry," he comforted as he sat beside me, holding my hand. "I'll think of something that makes them laugh on the other side of their face."

I was sure he would.

CHAPTER IV

The Old Gristmill

While I was sick, Blue did some exploring without Homer and me and made an exciting discovery, the city dump grounds. In a vague way we had always known the dump was there, but it took his description to make us realize what an interesting place it was. Rich folks threw away a lot of things that would be fun to play with. We decided to go and get some of them.

Saturday afternoon and Sunday after service were the only free time we had during the week. We chose Sunday as the better day for our expedition. It was forever coming.

Wednesday, Thursday and Friday dragged by. Saturday finally arrived. By early afternoon most of the weekend cooking was done, ready to be warmed up as needed. Double amounts of feed had been given the animals, and a double supply of wood piled in the box. Water was drawn and ready for Saturday night baths.

Our house we built of lumber discards from the sawmill. At one end was a raised dirt platform boarded around with barrel staves sawed in half. A large Red Cedar tub rested there, brass bound with a bung hole at one side. The water ran out of the tub through a v-shaped trough to the pig lot. Mama managed bath night as efficiently as she did all other projects. She got clean kids and wallow water for the pigs at the same time.

For baths, the cedar tub was first filled half-full of cold water, then warmed with pails of hot carried from the black wash pot. We took turns washing, with a little water run out and some fresh added after each bath. Our twin brother and sister bathed first. They were still babies and had no real opportunity to get dirty. The next cleanest came second, and so on. Homer and I were last. Bar soap and a "fine" shuck brush cleaned up right down to the bare perspiration glands. Had there been such a thing as deodorant, we would not have dared to use it. It would have burned like holy hallelujah hell.

I would have preferred to bathe myself, but I was made to undress and climb into the tub under the supervision of my older sister Anna. I hated the indecency of the whole process. Anna never missed a chance to poke fun at me.

"You back to normal after being so swelled up," teased Anna. "I can tell. You don't even raise the water an inch. Watch out now, or you'll go out the bung hole."

She laughed at her joke, and while she was laughing, Homer stuck a bar of lye soap in her mouth. She was afraid to tease much after that, but Homer got a prompt licking for wasting soap. I could tell by his eyes that it made just one more thing he was going to get even for when he had the chance.

The only remaining obstacle in the way of our freedom was church on Sunday morning. Our preacher was a long-winded old man who said all of real interest he had to say in the first five minutes when he read the scripture. Most of us knew his sermons by heart. He had learned only a few and gave them variety by presenting them in different manners. One Sunday he would shout hellfire and damnation, the next he would weep and tell it in a sad way, and the last he hissed and whispered. I amused myself by finding knots in the pine lumber and imagining what pictures they made. From time to time, I caught a little of the sermon, enough to know where the preacher was and how much longer I was going to have to sit still.

After church, Homer and I hurried through lunch and were ready for our adventure. Since the dump ground was several miles away through the woods, our discarded dirty clothes were a must. We changed into them in the wash house, hiding the Sunday best under the clothes basket.

Blue met us in the orchard, carrying a gunny sack. Homer and I brought some leftover lunch. We went hurriedly through the woods but carefully as well, especially when we came near a house or road. If anyone had seen us, the news would have gone swiftly back to Mama and Papa and Blue's parents, and lickings would have been waiting for us all around when we got home, we had not asked, but we knew very well that a trip to the dump grounds was not a permitted way to spend our free time Sunday afternoon.

When we arrived there, several people were busy dumping things. And we hid until the first wagon had gone. Then we ran to a spot which seemed to have lots of good usable items and began looking.

Homer and I started sorting through some old clothes, but Blue made the first important discovery. He turned over a wooden box, charred on one end, let out a squawk and jumped back like a jack rabbit. He motioned us to come and look. His face was pasty, and all he could say was, "She - - gar - - her woman." Holding hands, we crept over to see.

Homer stood and stared in astonishment. "Lord. Lord!" was all he said.

I gazed at the thing, my mind clicking as to its possible uses. It was the partially scorched head of a department store dummy. The hair was still in pretty good condition, but the wax face had melted askew. Homer picked it up gingerly and put it into Blue.

"We gonna scare the pants off some un," Blue said, eager to inflict his own fright on someone else. Homer and I agreed. In the orchard or a forbidden spot in the granary, we had often devised imaginary ways to be revenged of the people who gave us scoldings and lickings that we felt we did not deserve. We had fed them rat poison and put them in a dungeon of lions like the one brother Skaggs told about in church, but the head of the department store dummy promised a more satisfying solution. It was real.

Excited, we started back home with our head and various other discards, including an old dress from the pile of clothes Homer and I had first seen. Back in the wash house, we placed the head in a tub and washed it carefully. I combed the hair. She had been a beautiful dummy, and we handled it as if it were a live thing.

"I shore never seen anything like that 'fore," Blue said as we admired our find. Neither had Homer or I, but we never admitted ignorance of anything.

We discussed what to do and decided to use the dummy to scare our sisters as revenge on them for laughing at me and the calf. Blue proposed an oath that he said was sure to keep anyone from finding out our plans: "Never tell, never tell, or you're sure to go to hell." We swore ourselves to secrecy and felt safer in what we were doing.

All week we assembled the things we would need to set our stage, and the following Saturday afternoon we were ready. When Homer killed the chickens for Sunday dinner, he held one chicken by the feet and I squeezed the blood from the neck into a quart fruit jar. When our chores were done for the day, we took the blood and found some old eggs from a forsaken guinea nest. Then we picked up our head and the clothes from their hiding place and went to meet Blue at the spot we had selected for our plan.

Two miles from our house was a small gristmill. The former owner had lived upstairs in a loft room and done the grinding below. That way, his wife could help by releasing the primer pole without leaving her housework.

The mill had been abandoned a long time. Papa had tried to buy the site for his own new sawmill, but he and the owners had never been able to agree on a price.

While they dickered, the gristmill became more and more decayed. The old wheel revolved only when the creek flooded and only then with agonizing sounds. Dirt dauber wasps had built beautiful houses of clay in odd corners among the rafters.

We lugged our prize to this mill and arranged it as we had planned. With the calico dress from the dump and the waste cotton and shucks, we fashioned our "lady" until she was just right to our way of thinking. It really looked as though someone had hastily rammed her lifeless body into the closet and the door had swung open allowing the body to fall out in an unlikely position. It scared us and we knew what it was!

Satisfied at last, we hurried down the steep narrow steps from the loft room. The three of us enjoyed the pleasurable anticipation of our sisters' fright when they saw our handiwork the following day.

Sunday afternoon, Homer and I escaped for playtime as usual and ran down to the mill to put the finishing touches on our plan. We thinned the chicken blood with some of Mama's syrupy lye soap and poured it over the "corpse." Homer collected the guinea eggs which had matured considerably, and I climbed back to the lower floor, When I was safely down the steps, he tossed the rotten eggs into a far corner of the loft. Plop, plop, plop.

They burst with a noise like a popgun. Homer scrambled down the steps, and we waited at the bottom until we got a whiff of the result. It was awful.

We headed for home as fast as we could go, changed into our good clothes, caught our breath and wandered in among the family and their guests. Some were playing croquet and others singing hymns. My oldest sister and one of her beaus were sitting in the porch swing.

We quickly told our story.

Walking by the old gristmill, we had smelled something that stank awful. It smelled like it was upstairs. "Smelt like a dead thing," Homer said, and I nodded.

"We'd better find out about this," said Papa gravely. He took his bullwhip and started for the mill. He was an expert with that whip. He could clip the head off a snake in a single flash.

Everyone was curious to know what was going on. The entire group left their Sunday afternoon pursuits and headed for the mill behind Papa. Homer and I jogged along, listening to wild tales about the place.

Papa went in first when we reached the mill, followed by my older brother and one of my sister's young admirers. Homer and I accompanied them, eager to see the first success of our plan. In the tension of the moment, nobody thought to tell us to stay back.

"It smells like foul play," Papa said at the bottom of the steps.

"Smells like rotten eggs to me," said my older brother.

"Me too": chorused Homer and I. I doubt if anyone heard what we said.

Papa climbed the stairs carefully, testing his weight on each step. He took one look into the loft and said, "Two of you go into town and get Virgil. Take the horses that are saddled."

"Virgil's horse is lame, but he can ride one of yours back. One of you will have to stay in town."

Homer and I looked at each other, thrilled. Virgil was the sheriff.

Since there was nothing to do for the moment but wait, we went back out to join the rest of the family, congregated under the trees near the mill. Every once in a while a strong odor wafted its way down to us. Anna wanted to see what was in the loft. She climbed up and put her head over the landing, looked around and promptly fainted. Only the support of one of the young men behind kept her from tumbling down the ladder. Another beau felt a similar need to satisfy his curiosity and lost his chicken and dumpling dinner. Thereafter, the talk was all of two questions; who could it be, and who could have done it?

Homer and I became aware of a peculiar sound above us and looked up. High in the secluded branches of a mulberry tree was Blue, laughing fit to kill. We would have liked to do the same but did not dare.

Virgil must have made the distance out from town in record time. For it did not seem long until he came tearing down the road, his horse covered with sweat and dust. "What's the fuss all about, Uncle Bill?" he asked, puffing and wheezing, as he rode up. Like almost everybody in the county, he called Papa Uncle Bill.

"Well now, Virg, whatever it is, ain't no cause to kill a good horse." Papa was calm. "You young uns, rub that horse down and walk him in the shade there' til he cools down."

Virgil slid off the saddle and gave the reins to one of the Sutton boys. Homer and I giggled watching him. It looked as if he had wet his pants, his clothes were so soaked with sweat. He pushed his hat back from a freckled forehead and rubbed his face with a blue bandana.

There was little need for a sheriff in our county, and any work caused Virgil a great anguish of indecision. He shifted from one foot to the other not knowing what to do next. Especially about a murder. There had never been a murder while he was sheriff. Everyone else was aware of his predicament, a fact which did nothing to relieve his embarrassment. He cleared his throat.

"Well now, first off I got to ask questions. Who found this murder?"

"First off, Virgil, you had better find out whether there's a murder or not and then get to the questions." Papa was more in command of the situation than the sheriff was. He seemed to know it was up to him to see that Virgil kept his work in the proper perspective.

"Sure, sure," agreed Virgil. "Glad for the suggestion. I'll go have a look."

He placed his big ham of a hand on the bannister leading up to the loft. I was standing close, and I could see the long red fuzz covering the brown freckles on his hand. It trembled. Taking the pistol from an unaccustomed holster, carried loosely, he slowly mounted the narrow stairs.

A whiff of something rotten wafted by Virgil's nose and he turned white. He stood for a moment gulping, realized all eyes were focused on him, and turned back to give us a sickly grin. Then he lumbered on up the stairs. Feeling sorry for him, Papa followed closely with his bullwhip.

The dirt daubers buzzed angrily as Virgil walked gingerly toward the body, grunting and trying to keep from vomiting. He held his nose and turned the head in the dim light to see if he could identify it. His voice came suddenly from the corner of the loft, loud and relieved.

"Uncle, someone done played a trick on you. This here's an old dress stuffed with shucks and some bad guinea eggs broke around to make it natural like."

Virgil laughed and Papa joined him. It was a joke, a joke on everyone there except Homer, Blue and me. We were afraid now that we would be found out.

Virgil was kidded about solving a murder, his first one, so quickly, He swore he was going to make the person pay who played that trick on him. But it was all bluster.

I think Papa knew one of his own kids was involved, but he did not push the matter. In the end, he profited by the hoax. People called the old mill haunted afterward. He bought the site for very little and later built his new sawmill on the spot.

CHAPTER V

The Yearly Trip to Town

Homer and I were glad Papa decided not to investigate what happened at the old gristmill. If we had been found out, a dreadful punishment would have followed. We would have lost the privilege of going to town with the rest of the family. Papa made the trip fairly often to trade with the merchants and settle various business matters connected with his sawmill, but we younger children made the trip only once a year. For us, the trip to town was a great event, one we began looking forward to months before it arrived.

Not going to town would mean no treats and no share in choosing the store-bought clothes and shoes. It also earned us the anger of whichever one of our older brothers or sisters had to stay behind and keep us from getting into further mischief. Even Blue suffered from our punishment because we always shared our treats with him, and Homer smuggled him home cigar and cigarette stubs found on the streets. Once, only once, we had to stay home, and Anna made the experience so miserable that we promised ourselves it would never happen again.

The entire family was incorporated into preparations for the annual visit to town, and anticipation was at a fever pitch by the time all was in readiness. Thursday was a preparation day. Everybody had either one large job or several small ones.

The first chore allotted to Homer and me was preparing the baths for the entire family, a time-consuming job. We drew water and carried it, enough to fill a fifty-gallon wash pot. Then, we covered the pot with a piece of galvanized tin and started the wood gathering. We dragged oak limbs and pine-knots to the wash place and arranged them around the pot. It was not time yet to light the fire, but everything else was ready. The wash pot was a promise that the trip to town would really happen.

Papa helped and directed the older boys in the loading of the wagons. They placed fresh hay in the wagon beds for us to sit on and applied axle grease liberally to the underside of the wagons. We had to ford the river, and the grease helped keep the beds dry.

The lead wagon was filled with things to sell and trade for necessities: molasses, vinegar, brine meat in huge wooden barrels, dried fruit, tobacco bundles, smoked home-cured bacon and wild turkey, jars of jelly and jam especially prepared for trade. There were also willow chairs Papa made himself and furs he had taken in trade for grinding cornmeal and flour. When both wagons were ready, they were pulled around to the front of the house, another sign of the promised trip.

Homer and I were hardly allowed to stand idle when there was so much to be done. From one chore to another we worked side by side, sharing plans of what we would do when we got to town. We shucked and shelled corn, hauled pumpkins and pitched hay, filled water troughs and penned up the baby chicks. All day long, we ran here and there at everybody's beck and call.

With the help of our older sister, Mama baked a ham and a basket of sweet potatoes, boiled several dozen eggs, made dozens of fried pies, selected melons and fruit, and prepared jugs of water and buttermilk. She filled her "quick lunch" basket with molasses cookies and roasted peanuts to nibble on the way. We did not have to be careful with crumbs or hulls on the trip to town.

Two of the girls worked at getting the wardrobes ready, a complete outfit for each member of the family, the fresh linen darned and ironed and all the buttons sewed on. They also packed the first aid kit; needle, thread, scissors, shoe hook, a box of salve, strips of old linen and on top, the traveling Bible.

Thursday evening bath time started early. The fire around the pot was lit, and soon the water was boiling. As on Saturday, baths began with the littlest. We younger ones were fed, bathed, dressed ready to travel and put to bed.

At three in the morning we were sleepily moved from bed to the wagon and covered with warm quilts, and the journey to town began. The lead wagon moved out with a lurch. When it was well in advance, Papa clicked his tongue, and we started. Cotton Top and Blue Boy seemed as eager to take us as we were to go. Homer squeezed my hand, and the utter enjoyment of the occasion filled my being. I could not sleep. I was afraid I would miss something important.

After a few miles over the gully-washed roads, we were all awake. The red clay road was covered in places with wild roses, morning glory and honeysuckle. Flitting along as if greeting us were meadow larks and bank swallows. We chattered excitedly, happy in being allowed for once to talk and shout without being scolded. It was wonderful.

At sunrise, Papa stopped the wagons with a "Hey, ho!"

We pulled up beside the lead wagon. "Time for breakfast and prayers, boys," said Papa. I knew, as we all did, that this was Mama's idea. Nothing interfered with prayers.

We could understand a little better when we climbed down from the wagon and saw the river ahead of us. We stood around eating boiled eggs and drinking milk, then walked with Papa to the river's edge. Bowing our heads, we listened to Mama's clear voice, "Dear lord, we ask guidance in what we undertake. If it be thy will, see us safely to the other side of this river and this life. Amen."

"Amen," repeated Papa.

We started to scramble back to our places in the wagons. "Wait," said Papa. To Homer and me, he gave two nickels each, while the older girls got four nickels and the boys got fifty cents, which was a lot of money.

"Now, William," remonstrated Mama.

"Woman, no use to go to town without money." Papa smiled and lifted us into the wagon.

The money was exciting, but I was worried about something else, I tugged Homer's sleeve and asked, "How we Gonna get to town over that ol' river? It's high."

"You heard Mama," he whispered back. "God's gonna help."

I nodded, satisfied.

The river was not far from town. But it had to be crossed to get there. There was no bridge.

"Hold on to the wagon and each other." Papa cautioned. He knew the river well. Having forded it often, so he let the dray wagon follow him through. The river could be tricky.

We felt the smoothness when the wagon floated. We let our hands float on the water and splashed each other, giggling and beginning everything we said with "what if." What if we should all be drowned - - pleasant things like that.

The wagons eased through. Only a little water seeped into the beds. The mules pulled out on the far side, dripping and smelling of the sweetish, half-decayed river ooze.

As we drew nearer town, the day became warm. We were all getting really excited.

"Hear that ol' locomotive?" Papa asked suddenly. "Pulling a heavy load. Ain't that something?"

He lashed the team to bring us close enough to see. The train whistled loud and long. We were within a few hundred yards of the grade crossing as it whooshed by, dragging a long freight. Then, a passenger train steamed past going the other direction. Passengers waved. We waved back and yelled even though we knew they would not hear us.

"Trains make me sad," Said Mama with a sigh. I knew how she felt. Sometimes, a train gave me that feeling, the sad lonely feeling of being left behind.

The smell of coal smoke was the first hint we had that we were close to town. We took in every smell and sight and sound.

We passed the cotton gin where hundreds of bales of cotton were stacked on loading platforms beside empty boxcars. Black and white stevedores worked side by side skidding and loading, singing work songs as they swung the heavy bales into place. The men paused to return our wave, then continued their work. The smells of freshly ginned cotton and jute bags mingled with those of rich cotton seed oil, sweaty mules and oiled machinery.

Beyond the gin was the wagon yard, already alive with early arrivals for the Friday training. Babies cried, and dogs barked. A fight between two children earned them each a prompt scolding. The mothers involved had to show the other women in the wagon yard that they made their children mind.

We searched for and found a place to hitch the mules. Papa unhitched them from the wagon, tossed hay into a mow and spoke briefly with Mama before leaving with the dray. The older boys accompanied him.

Homer and I ambled around smug and smart until Mama ordered us to get the kindling and firewood from the wagon. I jumped nimbly into the wagon and handed down each piece, aware of the many eyes on me. I wanted to be seen, especially by the other girls, for I was wearing a new dress with lace around the collar.

For cooking away from home, Papa had made a tripod of iron. An old bread pan suspended from it by chains formed a tray in which Mama could set the coffee pot and a pan of vegetables with a pan of cornbread on top. When Homer and I set up this invention, Mama was the envy of all the women present, and she gloried in the whole thing. Homer and I acted like it wasn't so much, but we were proud, too.

After the last of our chores was finished, we were free to do as we liked until lunch. And we were eager to make the most of our opportunity. However, the children at the neighboring wagons were shy and ill at ease, so it took a while to make new acquaintances.

The arrival of the Steel family, our closest neighbors, changed that situation, and we were elated, Leon, the oldest of the Steel boys, was trusted to be fair about everything and took charge of trading among us children for that reason. There had to be someone to settle the quarrels about what was a fair swap. In a few minutes we were surrounded by boys and girls. All talking at once.

Trading was quite as important to us children as to the grownups, and it was conducted along the same lines, right down to the "to boot," the something extra which sealed a bargain. The items offered for trade were as varied as we were ourselves. There were tops, a thread spool for a hockey spinner, string included. There were slingshots, whistles made from willow and hickory limbs, and jump ropes cut from the end of a halter, cut just before departure, most likely. The Nabor kids were expert carvers and brought wooden figurines to trade. Iron hoops were a popular item, and the boy who offered them for trade pushed one through the wagon yard with it's guide lath, demonstrating all the fancy turns and spins it could be made to perform by a practiced hand. The girls had rag dolls, fans, beads made from china berry seeds, and carved heads from walnut and hickory nuts. I had brought some slick pages from the old catalogue. They were much in demand for paper dolls, and I was not scolded for taking them from the outhouse. The rough pages were more desirable for toilet paper.

When we wearied of trading and repeating the gossip we had been warned not to say a thing about, we began to look around for further entertainment. Maybelle Hoglin and her friend Nancy Baker had arrived and were keeping themselves very much at the center of things. Maybelle, especially, gave every sign of being pleased when the trading was over, as she wanted to attract the attention of Leon Steel to herself.

The tailgate of the Baker wagon had been let down, and both girls began showing off on it, pretending they had trouble climbing up and promptly falling off again as soon as they succeeded.

Maybelle dropped her handkerchief for Leon's benefit, and he picked it up and handed it back to her with poor grace. Homer and the other Steel boys imitated the performance. Homer played Maybelle's part, accepting an imaginary handkerchief from Willie Steel with a smirk.

Nancy and Maybelle loved every minute of it, though they acted as if they were offended. During one of their squealing episodes, I had an idea. I climbed up into the wagon and took the can of axle grease Papa always kept in the tool box. I stood holding it, waiting until Homer would notice me. I said nothing, just stood. Finally, he looked my way and realized instantly what I had in mind. I saw him explain it to one of his friends in a whisper.

Homer sauntered casually over to get the can of axle grease, and some of the other boys teased Maybelle and Nancy until the two jumped off the tailgate and started in pursuit of their tormenters. They threw small stones and sticks as if they were exasperated. While they were thus engaged, Homer and Ted Steel smeared axle grease all over the tailgate where Maybelle and Nancy would soon be sitting. Stifling laughter, we dispersed to watch the results from a safe distance

Pleased with themselves and their success at attracting the attention of the boys, Maybelle and Nancy flounced back to the Baker wagon. Eyes fastened on their admirers, they never once looked at the tailgate as they resumed their former seats. The slick surface warned them, but too late. They came down faster than they had climbed up, and Maybelle let out a shriek which brought Mrs. Baker to the scene in a hurry.

Nancy's mother was thoroughly disgusted when she saw the sticky black grease on their skirts. Maybelle got a licking in front of everybody, and Nancy was told she would have to sit in the wagon for the rest of the afternoon. She wept and pleaded but all in vain, "You should have looked," was her mother's only response. "You know how those boys are."

By the time this excitement had died down, it was time for the noon meal. Everybody was hungry, and the smell of campfires, frying ham and boiled coffee stimulated the appetite even for those a little off their feed from the combination of bustle and strange surroundings.

Mama let down the tailgate and spread a checkered cloth over the back part of our wagon. "I sure hope the Skaggs and Howards don't 'just drop by, '"she said as she placed dishes of vegetables and cornbread and fried chicken around. We hoped so, too. The Skaggs and the Howards could eat as much as the crew of Papa's sawmill, all by having a bite of this and that, "just to taste."

Papa soon returned. He was in a good humor, having disposed of the trade goods and received orders for several chairs and a cradle. He brought with him a number of men who had come to town without their families and had nowhere to eat lunch. There was plenty of food for all, and Mama made them welcome.

It was a wonderful meal to me. We children could splash or spill or drip. It didn't matter. This was one time we were never scolded, and the freedom made everything taste better.

Mama had found time during the morning to have copies of pictures made, and she passed them around at the end of the meal to have everyone admire them. They were of her holding the body of the dead baby tenderly in her arms, the baby she was always so proud of, the one whose place I would never be able to fill.

I had been eating a ripe peach, and when the picture was handed to me, I held it so the peach juice ran down on the baby's face. I did it deliberately, but Homer, seeing our afternoon spoiled if Mama noticed what I had done, snatched the picture and wiped it off with his shirt sleeve. He knew how I felt, but he also knew the penalty for wrongdoing.

He grabbed my hand and hissed, "You 'bout ruined everything! You can do that when we get home. You want to get a lickin' like that ol' Maybelle, <u>and</u> have to sit in the wagon like that Nancy Baker?"

I knew he was right, so I said nothing.

When the empty dishes from lunch had been packed away, Papa gave Mama a list of the merchants where he had traded, with the amount owing to him beside each name. Those were the places she could shop.

We went with Mama while she bought bolts of cloth, thread, ribbons, hooks and eyes. There were spices also; a bag full of whole nutmegs, cinnamon in two-pound boxes, chocolate in five-pound cartons, cans of coconut and baking powder. A clerk in the dry-goods store placed a wooden case of Arm and Hammer soda on the counter beside the sulphur, glycerine and rose water, and a complete suit of underwear for each member of the family. Mama also bought a keg of oatmeal and a large can of dry mustard for poultices. These things were always store-bought.

Papa had purchases to make also. He bought Star-Navy, Red Mule and Horseshoe chewing tobacco by the carton, several strips of shoe soling leather, boxes of tacks, saddle soap, strips of iron for the wagon and plow repairs, a keg of nails and charcoal for the blacksmith shop. In addition, he always got a new pair of bibbed overalls just for himself.

When Mama and Papa were through trading, we were allowed to shop for ourselves. A dime store then lived up to its name, and the wonders of that store were innumerable. Homer and I felt we owned the world with our two nickels apiece. I bought a four-inch china doll for two cents, a box of Chums with a lovely golden glass slipper as a prize, five jaw breakers for a penny, and a small bag of agates for Blue.

From the dime store, Papa took us to the soda fountain for a city treat. "This is an unheard of extravagance, William," said Mama as we stood in the door, but Papa led us all inside. It probably was extravagant, but it was also a joy supreme; ice cream and pink lemonade. It was cold and delicious in spite of the flat taste afterward.

After the treat, we went to Dr. Kelley's. As the only nurse for miles around, Mama worked with the doctor in his country practice, and the trip to town was an opportunity for her to receive his instructions about the care and medication of his patients in our locality.

Dr. Kelley had eight children, several of them just about the ages of Homer and me. Mama told us that while she was having her consultation with the doctor, we might go and play with them. "But don't you children get into any mischief," she cautioned. We nodded. That was not really a promise.

The doctor's children knew everything there was to know about living in town, every empty house and place of interest. "What you all want to do?" asked Homer, as soon as Mama was out of earshot.

Fred Kelley spoke up. "I got half a bag of Bull Durham. Let's go to the jail."

"Sure thing," said Home, and we were off.

The jail was a forbidden place for us, as we were told to steer clear of any signs of sin or wrongdoing, but Freddy, Ann and Jonnie assured us they went quite often. If they could get into the alley without Virgil seeing them, they could sell cigarettes and chewing tobacco to the inmates, sometimes for as much as a dime. We digested this information and began to scour the streets for cigarettes.

Virgil was nowhere in sight when we got to the jail. Ann, Jonnie and I let the boys take full charge of the project. They climbed up to the narrow barred window and hissed until whoever was inside heard them, but we were not very lucky this time. The inmates did not have a dime, not even a nickel. We decided to give them what tobacco we had and let that be our good deed for the day. Everything good which happened to us the rest of the afternoon was attributed to that good deed.

Virgil caught us as we were coming from behind the jail and gave us one of his most sheriff-like looks, but he did not press us for an explanation. When he walked on, we made faces and said some very unkind things behind his back.

Leaving the jail we met Leon Steel, and all six of us went in search of further adventure. When we got to main street, Homer glanced ahead and saw the mortuary. He nudged Freddy. "Hey, has ol' Ashbury got any dead uns?"

"Sure!" Freddy was enthusiastic. "Just this morning too, ol' Trolly Brooks. You all want to see?"

Everybody nodded.

We walked slowly past the mortuary our heads bowed as we thought benefitted a place devoted to the dead. Just beyond, we slipped into a crack between the buildings and headed for the alley.

The mortuary had what was to us an impressive white front with a large window over which hung a black curtain drawn back at the sides. The remainder of the frame building was somewhat like the owner: a lot in front and not much behind. What little was there was covered by a flat roof which slanted to within a few inches of the ground. Inside this lean-to were stored the extra coffins, a few old and often-used angels and some very faded silk flowers.

We squeezed into this storeroom through a small window at the back which was covered only with wooden shutters. It was a shivering delight. Not that we were curious about the dead, for lord knows we had to touch all the relatives who died and posed for pictures in which all present crowded as close to the coffin as they could. Those things were a custom, at least in our part of the country. No, it was the secrecy of the whole thing that gave us the thrill. We crept through the storeroom to the main part of the mortuary, Homer and Leon bent their backs, making a kind of platform from which each of us in turn could look through the little window into the room where the dead were kept.

Ann climbed up first to see if the coast was clear. "Jeddy! My gosh!" she exclaimed. "Lemme down!"

"What is it?"asked her brother, and Jonnie joined in with "What's you see, huh?"

"Ol' Trolly is just laying there." Ann took a deep breath. "But he's naked as a jaybird. Gosh all me, he ain't got nothing on. Nothing, I tell you."

She raised her skirt above her knees to show us what she meant, and we all snickered and giggled. Then the rest of us had a chance to look. My turn finally came.

Why such things always happened to me, I'll never know, but there I was standing straddle-legged on top of Homer and Leon, gaping at an old man I had seen many times before, when Mr. Ashbury opened the inside door and wheeled in another body. It was a woman. I almost fainted. He put her alongside of old Trolly, then actually introduced them.

"Trolly, meet Miz Ebby Patten. She lives out in shanty town, but she's a real nice lady. Accommodating, too. You can take my word for it. I been out to her place plenty of times myself." He lifted the foot end of the gray flannel thing that covered her and nodded. "Yep, Trolly, it's her all right. I'd know that ol' place anywhere." Then, he went to the head end and pinched Miz Ebby's cheek. "Nice of me to find someone to go along with you, now warn't it, Ebby?"

I slipped off Homer's back and came down with a bump. I did not usually say anything around people other than my brother and Blue, but this time I made an exception. "He's talking to them! Just like they were alive, he's talking. Sure as Satan, he's - - crazy. Let's git out of here!"

We scampered for dear life, knocking over some boxes in the process. We were out the window into the alley just in time. Mr. Ashbury came into the storeroom, and we stood outside holding our breaths until we heard him say, "Thought I heard something out here, Trollly, but it warn't nothin'. Not a thing to disturb you. I'll just leave you alone with Miz Ebby. Now, don't you do nothing wrong, you hear?"

When Mr. Ashbury went back to the front of the mortuary, we crept carefully around the corner of the building and ran for the chestnut tree on the courthouse lawn. There, breathless and giggling, I repeated to them what I had seen and heard.

The excitement of our adventure was still very evident when we got back to the doctor's house. Mama was waiting impatiently for us. "Where have you been?" she wanted to know, but before Homer could answer her, she added a quick, "Never mind. We have to go now."

We said our goodbyes, made plans for a return visit from the Kelleys and were soon ready to travel. Tired and happy, we settled down under our quilts in the wagon. Twilight gathered as Papa drove the mules homeward, and I lay awake listening to him talk with Mama about the day's events. In my last conscious moment, I heard Mama's voice, "Keep us safe, dear God." I knew we were crossing the river.

We smaller ones never knew when we arrived home. Papa or one of the older boys carried us up to bed. We were exhausted after our trip to town, but it was a happy feeling. We would discuss the trip for many months to come.

CHAPTER VI

Visiting Blue's Family

The day after the trip to town, my brother and I slipped off from home to give Blue the gifts we had gathered for him. We had a matchbox full. Homer and I had each contributed a jawbreaker. One of the "Top Notch" variety, and Homer had found a smooth crystal rock, the kind prized by Blue's family. We had several good-smelling gum wrappers, cigarette stubs and three cigar butts with the bands still on. Actually, we had picked up discarded bands and put them on, but we did not intend to tell Blue that. Most important of all, we had spent a penny for five Glassies. Pure glass marbles, brand new without a single nick or scratch.

We knew the way to Blue's house well, for we had been there many times, always without Mama's knowledge. We were acquainted with the whole Paradise family. There were seven of them: Pinkie and Popper, Blue's mother and father, his older sister Julia, a younger brother, a sister and his grandmother.

Granny Paradise fascinated me. Her hair was a snowy white like newborn lambskin, topping a shiny face of ebony, so wrinkled and seamed it looked sewn together. She constantly smoked rabbit tobacco or "homegrown" in a corncob pipe, and her lip full of powdered snuff. Her voice was melodious and soft but carried a tone for instant obedience. Her skirts swept the floor as she hobbled around with a crooked briar cane, knotty and polished. She almost always wore a blue print calico dress or waist, with skirt upon skirt. Each had deep pockets filled with magic and medicine of all kinds; buckeyes, powered roots, charm bags, a braid of hair from a dead person, a real tiger eye and rattles from a big rattler. Each article could curse or cure.

Julia, Blue's older sister, had attended school and worked as a maid in the home of one of the city bankers. She was a neat, well-built girl and clever. She carved the words "Pair - o - dice" on a bark-covered slab and nailed it above the gate of their house on a vine arbor. The people in our neighborhood thought she had just misspelled the name, but we knew she had done it that way purposely. She often referred to her mother and father jokingly as a pair of dice. When food was scarce, they were a poor Pair - o - dice, but when things changed for the better, they were rolling the right way. Homer and I looked for Julia's sign as we approached Blue's house.

The house, all two rooms of it, stood in the middle of a cleared field. Along the back was a kind of porch framed with poles and roofed with palmetto fronds and brush, It was a stall for the family donkey, and the house itself formed one wall of his pen, while the other three sides were enclosed by a cane fence woven with various oddments of wire, jute string, old rags and wild grapevine.

Dooley Donkey paid no attention to my brother and me as we walked along the outside of his cane fence. He was standing near the house looking through the window, but we thought nothing of that at first glance. He usually stood there, watching for any handout the kids might shove his way.

Homer began to whistle "Ol' Dan Tucker" loud and clear to signal Blue. We walked on quietly, listening for his response of "Dig Big 'Tators," but it did not come.

"Wonder what happened," I said.

"I don't know," Homer shrugged. "Maybe something goin' on inside. Keep down, and don't say a word if they catch us. I'll do the talking."

We clambered over the cane fence and crept up to the back window to see what we could find out. Homer pushed an old wooden crate over to the window and shoved the donkey to one side. I climbed up beside my brother.

There before our eyes was Paradise, the whole darn kit an kaboodle, except for our friend Blue. His mama and papa were standing beside a bulging tow sack which hung from a peg. They were actually talking to it, telling it that it had better mend the error of its ways.

"Must be some kind of Blue's magic like he talks 'bout," whispered Homer. I could feel him trembling. "Maybe we better git from here fast."

"No," I protested, "Let's see what they do. May come in handy sometime when we most need it."

Blue's father interrupted us, rumbling another threat at the sack. "You gonna stay in there 'till judgment day if'n you keep telling us lies. You 'ont that ol' debble take you plum down into hell? Hit's a lot hotter in hell than it is in that sack."

The bulge in the sack wiggled. Blue's voice came tearfully from inside. "I wan' otta here, Pa. I done learned my lesson. I done truly learned my lesson."

Shocked, Homer and I stood agape, peering through the window. We had often heard Blue say that he was going to "git sacked" if he did such - and - such, but we had attached no great significance to the expression. Today, our eyes had been opened.

"Pa," pleaded Blue from inside the sack.

"You sure you done learned your lesson?"

"Yes, Pa."

"All right then."

Relenting, Popper Paradise lifted the sack down from the peg. And Blue's mother untied an old cotton stocking used to hold it shut. Out crawled Blue, sweating and covered with jute fuzz. Tears ran down his cheek, and he stood naked as the day he was born.

"There you is." declared Granny Paradise, hovering over him with a wet rag. "You in the same tracks you gonna be in come judgment day, when you has to stand 'fore God and sah, I done told a lie, God. And 'member this chile, it gonna feel good, like this cloth I done wrung out cool water when God say, Blue, I forgives you." She gently swabbed off the sweat and jute fuzz. Then with a chuckle and a flick. She popped him with the wet cloth.

Released, Blue grabbed his clothes and was out of the house like a shot, pumping his legs into the worn-out overalls that covered his shoulders better than the rest of him. We dropped to the ground and ran to join him.

"What happened?"

"Why the sack?"

"They put you in there much?"

We asked questions faster than Blue could answer. He took the last one first. "Gar, I done told a whopper, and I got the sack for it. Pure luck I didn't git salt in the sack."

My eyes widened. "You mean that sack gits salt in it too, when they punish you?"

"You betcha. It works good, too. I ain' told one in a long time 'til now. I say I ain't been to the Craxton place, and ol' Craxton told my pa I took the rabbit outta his trap. How was I to know he was watchin' that trap? Stingy ol' man!"

"But Blue," said Homer, trying to be reasonable, "it was his trap, and he has to eat, too."

"Not that rabbit, he don't." Blue was adamant. "She got a whole nest of little uns. I seen her wid 'em. She got a skunt place on her back, and I know it's the same mama rabbit, so I turned her loose."

"Oh ," Homer nodded, understanding. "You done right, but why not tell your folks that?"

"Cause it was his trap caught that rabbit, and I am got no sin on me for what he does."

"Well, no use to worry over it," said Homer, changing the subject. "Here's some thing we brought you from town. Maybe make you feel better."

My brother handed over the matchbox, and we stood watching the expression on Blue's face as he opened it. His indignation about the rabbit was slowly replaced by a grin, and he ducked his head. Then to hide how he felt, he pushed Homer and hit me on the shoulder. It was a thank you we understood.

"Pa, he gonna love this ol' bacca," said Blue. "And he gonna feel real bad that he sacked me when I give it to him." He smiled at the thought.

After our gifts had been presented and accepted, we three sat astride the tie pole near the side of the house. Since it was part of his pen, the donkey ambled over to us and nudged Blue affectionately.

Blue pushed back. "Gwan! Can't you see I'm rich?" He held up a marble. "See, you ol' mule? My friends done made me wealthy. Ain't none of the folks I know got no agate."

Opening the matchbox, Blue put his glassy back in a safe place. That accomplished, he asked us what we had seen and done in town, and we were glad to tell him everything. As we were describing our encounter with Virgil at the jail, Blue's mother called to us from the window.

"You all come on in and eat your supper."

Homer and I looked at each other, uncertain whether or not the invitation included us. "You mean my sister and me?" asked Homer.

Pinky smiled and nodded. "Sure, Sure."

"Come on," urged Blue. "Us gonna have some opossum."

We followed him inside more to see what would happen than anything else. While the Paradise children set the table, Homer and I stood just inside the cabin door examining the wonders of the room we had entered. It was a crowded place, used as bedroom, living room kitchen and dining room. Two beds separated only by a narrow space filled the back of the room. The mattresses were hay and shuck, each with a featherbed on top, covered with patchwork quilts made from old clothes carefully washed, ripped and stitched together with fine small stitches.

The walls were papered with newspaper clippings, pictures with captions and comics. "Happy Hoooligan," "Bringing up Father" and "The Katzenjammer Kids," were plastered beside the fireplace where you could read them while you were cooking or getting warm. Brown snuff bottles lined the mantel and held in place a broken plate Blue had found at the dump the day we three explored it. He had brought it home and presented it to his mother, for it was chipped on only one side and had beautiful flowers in the center.

Pinky carefully removed it from its display position and wiped off the dust. Turning to me, she said, "You can eaten from it, ain't it pretty?"

I nodded and thanked her.

We children sat on a long bench nailed on the wall while the grownups used various chairs. From my place at the table, I could see into the other room which held three beds much like those in the main room but less fluffy. Two sacks had been sewn together to form screens around the beds. It all seemed homey to me, friendly and comfortable. I glanced again at the comics covering the wall beside the fireplace.

"You all sure got a nice home," I said.

The sincerity in my voice was unmistakable. Granny Paradise beamed at my compliment. "You got a eye, gal. Yessir, that gal sho' got a eye."

"God and your daddy been real good to us," agreed Pinky, as she brought the food over from the hearth. The aroma from baked possum, fresh turnip greens, cornpone and baked sweet potatoes drifted around the table. My brother and I were each given a two-tined fork with a bone handle, the only ones like that. All the others were some kind of dark metal.

When Pinky served Homer, he looked at the full place set before him, then me, "Man alive," he said. "That sure does look scrumptious."

I nodded. It even looked that way to me, and possum was not my favorite food. When Mama or the older girls cooked it, I usually had a very bad "spell" beforehand, so I would not be able to eat.

Blue's mother brought her own plate last and sat down at the table. Popper nodded at Granny Paradise, and she began a short but fervent prayer.

"Deah God, we 'preciate the good vittles you done seen fit to help us git, and bless these little children who come to share 'em with us, fo'give them what needs fo'giving. God, Blue ain' no bad boy, but just like the rest of us, he forgit. Help him 'member the sack and why for it be used. Make this ol' possum taste like manna from heaven, and give us our strength so we can work and pray and be glorifying our Lord. Amen!"

We repeated the amen and started on the possum. Pinky had cooked by her own worked-out recipe, and after a few bites I knew it tasted as good as it smelled. I asked her how she make it taste so much better than Mama's. "Well, chile, I tell you. The most important is to start right. First, I dip ol' possum quick in hot water, like for scraping a hog. Hair it just slip off. Then I quick gut him and drop him in a pail of good hot sody water. If'n you don' have sody, just put wood ashes, a lot in some good hot water, and when it done settled, pour it off real careful. Leave ol' possum in that lye. I washes him clean in salt water and wrenches him in clear cold water, dries him and rubs him with salt and pepper and a mite of sage and bay leaves. I stuffs him up with sweet taters to slop up the grease, 'cause he greasy, and I bakes him in my oven right there on the hearth. It take awhile, and you gotta change the coals, keep 'em hot and sizzling. He done eat so many of your mom's chickens, he burn in hellfire just like the Good Book tell us. You sin, you burn. Ain't no tuckin or taking. When he brown like he is now and tender to pieces, you all just hep yourself. Sit back and eat right down to the bone. 'Cept, you best save a bit for ol' houn' dog what done treed that possum, or he's gonna go bad on you, and that's a fact. I done seen it happen many times."

I nodded. I knew Pinky was right because I had heard Papa say the same thing. Hound dogs would refuse to hunt unless they got a share of what they treed. We had eleven ourselves, and my older brothers were always careful to give them a taste of any raccoon or opossum killed.

Popper Paradise told about how he had lost the best hound dog he ever owned, and from there he, Homer and Blue went on to talk about the various dogs in the county and wether or not they were any good. I was proud of how much my brother knew on the subject. By the time they decided that Mr. Long's Delfeaser was probably the best there was, at least for coon, the opossum and greens were mostly gone.

After we ate all of the table food, Pinky brought in big persimmon cookies cut with an iron cutter that Popper had made in the blacksmith shop at the sawmill. One cookie apiece was enough for dessert, and she shooed us kids away from the table when she had handed them out. "I wanna thank you, Pinky," said Homer, acknowledging the unforgettable dinner before we started home. "That sure was the bestest dinner I ever did eat in a long while. You are a <u>good</u> cook." He rubbed his stomach contentedly.

"Me, too," I said. I was not sure I would be able to eat the cookie, I had eaten so much possum.

"We sure do thank you," repeated Homer. "But we best be gitting home now. Mama'll be looking for us."

Granny Paradise had left the table and taken a seat on a worn-down hickory slatted stool near the open fireplace. She crooked a finger at me, "fore you go, come here, gal."

Not knowing what to expect, I went over and stood in front of her. She did not say anything else to me right away. She sat on her stool rocking gently back and forth, her eyes squinting and opening, rolling and closing, while she hummed a rhyme under her breath.

"Gonna do a frien' a favor.

Gonna do it today.

Gonna weave me a magic.

Gonna take a corn away.

Wrap a hair from her head.

A nail from her toe.

Gonna hide in the night.

Ol' wart gonna go."

Hearing the word "wart," I glanced at my hands, the right one holding the persimmon cookie and the empty left one. I had a wart on my left hand. Mama had tried different remedies to make it go away, but so far none had worked.

I had just time to wonder if Granny Paradise was going to use one of her charms to cure my wart, when she grabbed me by the arm and quick as scat somehow made the wart on my hand bleed. I stood as though mesmerized, Unresisting. She turned to Pinky and said, "Daughter, gi' me a corner of yo' dish rag."

Without question, Pinky ripped off a small piece of some rag used to wash dishes and calmly handed it to Granny who dug into one of her numerous pockets, found a bag of reddish powder and sprinkled a little on my wart. Mumbling over and over the rhyming chant, she jerked several hairs from my head, crossed them carefully on the piece of rag and sprinkled a tiny bit of the powder on the exact center of the hairs.

"Now chile," she said looking directly at me. "Gotta have a nail. Daughter, cut the nail from the toe nearest the big toe, cut from lef' to right."

I looked calmly down at my bare feet while Pinky did as she was bid. I felt as if I had no part in it at all. Granny took the toenail and laid it carefully on top of the hairs. She tied the corners over the first and tied a knot so tight it almost burst the rag.

"Here chile," she said, placing the rag in my pinafore pocket "Take this charm, and tonight at twelve o'clock, you put it under a stone at the east end of yo' home. Say over and over three times:

Gonna weave me a magic.

Gonna take ol' corn away."

"Yo' brother knows bout the spell, but best not tell yo' folks, yo' mama special."

I nodded to show her I understood, and the movement seemed to shake off the sort of trance I had been in. I walked over to my brother and took his hand. As If he too, had been immobilized, he seemed to come to life.

"We better git," he prompted. "Mama's gonna be real mad if we don't git home 'fore supper."

I turned and looked at the members of the Paradise family. They had never appeared so distinct to me before. Each person, each item in the cabin was clearly pictured as if cut out and placed separately in space. With the courtesy usually reserved for relatives we wished to impress, I nodded toward each person and said politely, "I thank you for your hospitality and - - ," I looked down at my hand, "and help."

Every face had a smile for me.

I left the Paradise house with complete faith in Granny's cure, but on the way home doubts began to creep in. I was still sure the charm would get rid of my wart if anything could, but I was afraid I might not be able to do all the things that were necessary to make it work. Besides, the charm might do something to me beyond just take off a wart. I shared my fears with my brother.

"Homer, if we let one peep out 'bout this all, we gonna git the living tar beat outta our hides. An how'm I gonna git up at twelve midnight, huh?"

"Don't fret. I'll wake you. You'll see,"

I could tell from the sound of Homer's voice that he was as scared as I was. We might go to hell for listening to "Cures" or "Curses" which was the way most people referred to anything they were not too sure about. I did not say any more about that possibility on the way home.

Having eaten a sumptuous dinner at Blue's, Homer and I were not hungry for supper at home. Mama attributed our lack of appetite to the trip to town the day before, so we were sent to bed early, immediately after evening prayers.

I kept my fingers crossed during prayer time, I hated the ugly wart on my hand and had resolved to risk going to hell to get rid of it. I had a horror of getting them all over me, like in pictures of witches I had seen. I had thought it all through and decided that if I did become a witch I would be a do good witch, and never put a curse on anyone. When I had made this promise to myself with my fingers crossed at prayers, I felt much better.

Clutching the knotted rag in my pocket, I kissed Mama goodnight and said, "That was a nice prayer, Mama."

She jerked me off my feet as she pulled me towards my bed

"Now what devilment have you been up to, I wonder," she said, tucking me in. She did not wait for an answer.

As I lay on my pillow, I wondered, too. How?

Just how did mothers always know when you had done something they felt you shouldn't have? I was still puzzling over it when I fell asleep.

"Ressie! Ressie, time."

I awoke with a start. Homer was hissing in my ear and I needed no second urging. Quickly, I climbed from between the two sisters with whom I slept, saying, "I gotta use the chamberpot." I fairly ran down the long dark hall and outside.

Homer waited by the door for me. Although scared. I was determined. Before dark, I had placed a small garden shovel by the east step, and I retrieved it now. Expecting ghosts or the devil, anything, if I looked around. I dug the hole and recited the part of the charm Granny Paradise had told me to say. I had been afraid I would forget it, but the words came easily.

Gonna weave me a magic.

Gonna take ol' corn away.

I said it over three times. Placed the rag in the hole and pulled a rock over it. I also turned around three times, which was something we did to protect us, though from what I cannot remember. That done, I dashed back into the house where Homer waited.

"I did it," I panted. "Let' get to bed."

"Good night," whispered Homer, and we were soon both asleep, lulled by the magic of the night.

The wart actually did begin to grow smaller, I knew, for I watched it carefully. One day after a swim in the creek, I sat on the bank scratching my arm from a mosquito bite and happened to look at my hand. The wart was not there at all. There was no sign of it but a small particle of skin which came loose when I rubbed it. I yelled for Homer and Blue.

"Come see! It's gone. I mean it's really gone."

Blue looked at my hand, full of pride, "I knowed it," he said. "Granny sho' 'nuff know her wart stuff. She kid do mos' anything, give her time."

Homer met my eyes and asked seriously, "You gonna show it to Mama?"

I shrugged. "I dunno. I think I'll just let her find out all by herself. Then, she'll think it was the stuff she rubbed on it made it go away. Anyway, I've made up my mind. I'm gonna learn all Granny's charms and spells and curses. I'm gonna be just like her."

"Oh boy!" Homer was enthusiastic. "We can hex anybody we don't like."

Blue looked shocked. "Hol' on! You all white folks. You can't fool 'round with hexing. It too - - - too - - ." He groped for a word that would not come.

"Course," said Homer firmly. "That's why she's gonna learn. All the good uns anyway."

Blue still shook his head doubtfully, so I did not press the matter, but that did not change how I felt. My mind was made up. I was going to be someone special, someone who knew how to do things, just like Granny paradise.

CHAPTER VII

By a Thread

One morning at breakfast, Papa and Mama had an unexpected and not altogether welcome announcement for us. We were going with Mama on a visit to her folks in Georgia. We would take the train, and since trains were expensive, there was no point in making the visit a short one. We would stay several months, at least three, perhaps four.

I stared down at my plate of hot biscuits and gravy. Three months was a long time to spend with strangers, especially if they should take a dislike to Homer and me the way Miss Harris had at school.

Mama cleared her throat to attract attention. When I looked up, she was glaring at me, making it plain that I was her major problem, the only one among her thirteen children who was not a normal active youngster, safe to be shown to the family.

"You will have to behave yourself," she said in a strained voice that testified to her vexation, "and since you are so set on not talking, you can keep absolutely quiet."

Gazing steadily back at her, I said politely, "Yes, ma'am." I think she would have slapped my face if the table had not been in the way.

Immediately after breakfast our household was thrown into a turmoil. Three large trunks were hauled down from the attic, aired and polished. One was packed with baby clothes, the others with garments for the rest of us. Mama was careful to leave room for gifts and exchanges that were expected along the visitation route.

The preparations were tiring, and many times I slipped off to my secret resting place in the wash house where I could think things out. Over and over, the question came back to me; why did I have to go? Mama didn't really want me along on the trip, and Papa was staying behind with the older girls. Why couldn't I stay too?

Then, a Something that always seemed to help me out of my difficulties whispered, "Go Ressie. You'll meet new people and see new worlds. It's like the adventures in the "Third Book" at school, only real. Don't be afraid, go on."

Encouraged, I began to think of what might be good about the visit and promptly thought of the stove. Three months away in Georgia would be three whole months that I would not have to bring in the wood for Mrs. Blackie. Delighted at the idea, I fairly flew up the back steps into the kitchen and kicked the stove soundly to show her what I thought. It was a mistake. She kicked back. I had broken my toe.

I screamed, and everyone came running. "What happened?" demanded Mama.

Afraid to tell her the truth, I looked down at the kitchen floor and caught sight of the door prop. In the confusion, I was able to move it a few inches from its accustomed place. Then, pointing to the heavy sweet gum post, gnarled and twisted into almost human shape, I set up a fresh wail of agony.

"I - - stubbed my toe!"

"I knew it. I knew it!" Yelled Mama, shaking me by the arm. "I knew if there was any way you could bring me grief, you'd do it. Look at you! How many hundred times have you been up and down those steps, and you never stubbed your toe on that door prop before. I wouldn't be surprised to learn that you did it on purpose."

She went on scolding and shaking me, but it was no help. My toe still hurt, and it was fast becoming swollen. Finally, Mama calmed down enough to examine it. She splinted it and had Papa carve a wooden protector out of soft pine. I had to wear one old shoe and one new one, but Mama made it clear that nothing could interfere with her trip home.

One good thing about the toe, it did get me out of selling my chickens to Old Man Payne several days later. Someone else caught them and put them in his wire cage. My foot was better by then. I could walk on it pretty well, but I couldn't run fast enough to catch chickens.

After the peddler was gone, Mama found she needed a certain color and size thread. She called Homer and me in to instruct us in what she wanted and started us on our way to Payne's house. She thought he would be at home, since he had just bought the chickens and two calves.

Homer and I were plain scared as we closed our front gate behind us and started toward Payne's. It was a long, hot dusty three miles by road, but that was not what deterred us. We were well aware of the stories about Mrs. Payne. She was a witch. She kept a cat on her shoulder. She had a wolf for a watchdog. And her eyes could see in the dark, even into your mind.

We had built up such wild ideas before we were anywhere near the place that it was all we could do to go on, but we did. Mama's lickings were worse than anything we had ever heard of Mrs. Payne doing.

The Payne house was not on the road. A lane led back to it through dense woods. At one time, no doubt, it had been a very well kept place, but trees, vines and brush now obscured it from the eyes of passers by.

Homer took my hand. As we started down the wooded lane, he found a heavy stick. "Ain't nobody gonna hurt you, you'll see," he assured.

He spoke bravely, but I sensed he was as frightened as I was. I knew that in some way I had to inspire him with courage. Having had time to think it over, I felt we should discover for ourselves what a witch woman was like.

"Wait here a minute, Homer," I said, stopping where sand was ankle deep in the lane. "If Mrs. Payne is a witch, we are like Hansel and Gretel, and they got away, so I'll bet there ain't nothing for us to be scared of. And ain't Granny Paradise our friend? She'd know to fix anything that Mrs. Payne does to us. I can see how it'll be, and I can see things plain, plainer than people who talk a lot, now can't I? Let's walk up bold and say our say. The folks know where we are. They'll come looking if we don't get back."

I closed my eyes and squeezed Homer's hand tight. "God go with us," I repeated three times and finished with, "Now then, let's go."

We walked resolutely through the tangled woods into a small cleaning surrounding the house. There was no peddler's wagon in sight, only the dilapidated house with a few out buildings and a big, rough-coated dog over by the pig pen. He was whimpering and acting funny, like he was trying to get through the board fence and in with the pigs. Then, we heard a weak cry from that direction and forgot to be afraid in our curiosity to find out what was wrong.

We climbed the board fence enclosing the lot where several razorbacks were penned, and the sight that met our eyes was awful. Mrs. Payne had been caught and dragged down by the hogs. She was on her knees in the trampled muck one arm hanging stiff and almost useless at her side. Blood trickled steadily from her nose and oozed from cuts on her face. It was smeared where she had tried to wipe it off, and her tears made clean streaks through the drying blood.

"How'd you all git in there?" asked Homer, wide-eyed.

"He - - threw me," mumbled Mrs. Payne.

"Your husband?"

"That's right. For the hogs, but he didn't wait to see 'em start. He went on." Mrs. Payne looked at us, but her eyes were so vacant I wondered if she really saw us.

Apparently, the razorbacks had been frightened off by our approach. They were standing in a group on the far side of the pen, watching Homer and me, but it did not take them very long to decide we were no threat. They started back toward Mrs. Payne. Homer jumped down into the pen to pull her to safety while I picked up a smooth pole that was leaning against the fence and jabbed it at the nearest hog.

I got his attention right away. He squealed, and that drew the others. They milled around me, squealing and spattering pig muck as high as where I sat on the fence. I kept jabbing at them with the pole to make them stay back.

The razorbacks stayed interested in me long enough for my brother to help Mrs. Payne up onto the hog trough and over the fence. Once outside, her legs refused to take her any further and she lay on the bare ground, just breathing, not even trying to ger up. The wolfish dog nuzzled her, whimpering and licking her face.

"He threw me in the pen," she moaned. "Said I wasn't worth feeding except to the hogs. Said the hams might not be fit to eat, but he'd risk it."

We brought water from the well, washed her face and hands, and helped her back into the house. She used only one room and the kitchen. It was stacked with oddments of every kind. Several cats meowed and hissed as we struggled to get her into her chair and brought a low stool for her feet.

While Homer built a fire in the crumbling fireplace and put a tea kettle on the crane, I gave Mrs. Payne a good look. The piercing quality of her green eyes was the only thing witch-like I could see about her. Her hair was a reddish gray that showed signs of having once been rich auburn, and she wore it bunched on top of her head and pinned with thorns from a thicket behind the house. She held on to my hand as if she would never let go. She kept saying over and over, "Little one, God bless you. Once I had a little one like you."

She talked as if she was starved for the sound of a voice, even her own, and we asked questions as fast as we could.

"Mama sent us over to buy thread," explained Homer. "She don't have the right kind like she needs."

Mrs. Payne shook her head. "That will be in the storeroom, and my husband got the only key there is, wears it on his watch chain instead of a watch. He ain't here and I couldn't tell you when he's coming back. He done left me to die, and just 'cause I asked for some meal and flour. All I got to eat is greens. Used to be I didn't have to ask. Used to be I could get in that old storeroom any time, but - - -."

The idea of getting in the storeroom seemed to revive Mrs. Payne. She sat up straighter in her chair. "Won't neither be so hard to get in there. Will you children help me?"

Homer and I both nodded in agreement. "But ain't your storeroom locked?" cautioned Homer.

"Sure it is, but that don't make no difference. We can get in there if you'll help me."

The word "we" threw me for a minute until I realized Mrs. Payne was only going to tell us where and how to get in, not go with us herself. She rose from her chair and hobbled over to a barrel covered with old quilts where several kittens nestled. Moving them gently and mumbling some kind of talk to them, she reached down into the barrel and pulled out a long coil of rope. Turning, she grinned toothlessly.

"He ain't so smart as he thinks he is," she said with a smacking sound, as if she was eating something tasty. "Fore I got all broke in pieces, I used to climb in that old storeroom myself. He never knew. He never had no idea. Thought it was all pack rats."

She handed my brother the rope and went to a cupboard for a candle and matches which she gave to me. Thus equipped,, we left the kitchen and headed down a little-used path. She called the dog to follow us and a good number of cats came as well, appearing from every direction.

The storehouse was an old log barn built tight. It had a loft floored with thick heavy boards. Homer climbed into the loft by the vent window. I climbed up after him. Mrs. Payne tied a hammer in an old apron along with the rope, and my brother pulled it up into the loft. We found a board that from all evidence had been loosened before and finally succeeded in making an opening large enough for me to go through.

My brother tied one end of the rope securely around me and fastened the other end to a rafter. I was scared silly until he told me this was an adventure.

"It's like Aladdin gits let down in where the treasure is, only I wouldn't leave you down in this here storeroom for nothing. Not if there was rubies in there. Just do like I tell you, and you'll be all right."

That was good enough for me. I wiggled through the gap in the floor of the loft, and Homer eased me down carefully into utter darkness. I would have been scared of this had it not been a real secret adventure. At last my feet touched the floor of the storeroom, and the rope went slack. Homer's voice came from the opening above me.

"Light the candle, and stick it onto a good place like I showed you."

One match was all I needed for the candle. There were no drafts in that tight log barn.

What can you see?" asked Homer from the loft.

"Sausage, cloth, canned stuff." I called things out as I turned. "Dried apples and peaches. Sacks and sacks of cornmeal and flour." My eyes lighted suddenly as I spied a china figurine about four inches high resting on top of a dusty barrel. "And there's a doll down here, a nice china one with a painted yellow dress and black hair."

"Look for Mama's white thread," advised Homer. He was not ecstatic about that doll the way I was. "Put the thread in your apron pocket. You done that? Then tie a sack of dried fruit on the rope."

With a few regrets, I turned away from the doll and did what he said. The sack of fruit disappeared into the loft, and soon the rope dangled back empty.

"Now, tie on a sack of flour," instructed Homer.

Twenty-five pounds of flour was hard for me to handle, but I managed.

"Some sausage, then canned stuff."

I was tying the last thing onto the rope when I heard Mrs. Payne hollering from outside the storeroom. "Snuff! Please, I want some snuff."

As I put the snuff in my pocket, I spied the doll again. I sure wanted that doll, and I was doing something nice for Mrs. Payne. She really ought to do something nice for me.

"You ready?" called Homer.

There was not going to be time to get the doll. I tied the rope around me. Like I had around the dried fruit and the flour, and told my brother I was ready. He started to pull me up. The rope went tight, and my feet left the floor.

Suddenly, I realized I had forgotten the candle. I twisted around to look at it, and the adventure almost came to an end. The knot which had been secure enough for the flour could not take the strain of a wiggling girl. It parted, and I fell with a crash.

"Ressie, you all right?" came Homer's voice, and when I did not answer immediately, his face appeared in the opening where we had pried up the board.

"Yes, I think so," I said and got carefully to my feet to make sure I was telling the truth.

"That's fine," reassured Homer. "That's just fine. Now you stay right there, and don't be scared. I'm going to pull up the rope and tie a loop in it with a good knot. Then, I'll let it back down, and you

90

can put the loop around you. You won't fall then when I pull you out. All right?"

I nodded, and his face disappeared from the opening. The rope slithered up into the loft. I would have time to get that doll after all. I picked it up and put it in a different pocket from the one which held Mrs. Payne's snuff. It just fit.

When the rope came back down, I was ready indeed. I fitted the loop around my chest under my arms and blew out the candle. Foot by foot, Homer hauled me out. Then he nailed the board back, lowered me to the ground outside and climbed down from the loft himself.

It was getting late by that time. Homer and I carried the things from the storehouse back to Mrs. Payne's kitchen, and we made her as comfortable as we could, putting food and water in easy reach of her chair. Then we left, taking with us Mama's thread and the doll.

Homer and I were almost as scared on the way home as we had been coming over. What could we tell Mama about the doll? It was new, beautiful china, without a single crack, and Mama would know we hadn't bought it.

We decided it was too nice to throw away, and we couldn't tell about stealing it from Mrs. Payne, so we made a wide detour and came back to our house through the apple orchard. My brother quickly climbed our favorite tree and placed the doll in a knothole we used for various secret maps and other things we made. Knowing it would be safe there and not be found, we went on up to the house.

"We have to tell Mama about Mrs. Payne," I said. "But first I have to ask God to forgive me about the doll. Please God, I'm sorry I took the doll. I'll return it, Amen. Now lets go tell Mama."

Homer gave Mama the thread and spoke of Mrs. Payne. Mama took long enough from her mending and packing to compliment us on helping the old lady. She said it was the part of being a good Christian. I doubt she would have called it that if she had known about the doll. Homer let me explain to Mama how I held the pigs off while he dragged and pushed Mrs. Payne over the fence. Mama was so angry she forgot to say anything except, "I'll take care of this."

She did, she informed Papa. Papa made visits to the neighbors and the men folk watched for Mr. Payne to return home. We watched and waited too. Homer and I were hidden near the Payne house in a thorn brush growth. Papa explained their visit and informed Mr. Payne that the women folk were taking over to see about his wife's safety. All Mr. Payne could say was, "Ah,- Ah,- Ah,-Ah,- - - - - !" As the men said goodbye and left, Papa told Mr. Payne that Virgil would be informed. I left the doll on the back porch, breathed a sigh of relief and Homer and I went on back home. Mr. Payne must have come around because we heard no more complaints.

CHAPTER VIII

All Aboard

After that, the preparations for Mama's trip went smoothly right up to bath time on the day before our departure. Anxious to have everything just the way she wanted it, Mama supervised the process herself instead of leaving it entirely to Anna. When Homer's turn came, she gave the top of his head a sudden glare, picked something out of his hair, dropped it on the floor and stepped on it.

"How disgusting!" she said. "Lice! I don't know why that teacher let those filthy Walker children come to school. This is what was bound to happen." She turned to glare at me. "And I suppose you have them too. You were born to be a trouble to me. Anna! Bring me the scissors."

As soon as my older sister brought the scissors, Mama made short work of the lice problem. She cropped Homer's hair off as close to the scalp as she could work the scissors and tossed the clippings into the fire under the wash pot. My turn came next. While I held my nose at the smell of burning hair, Mama snipped and wacked until a few uneven brown tufts were all that kept me from being completely bald.

Anna snickered at the result. "How you going to hide <u>her</u>, Mama?" she asked. "The trunks are all three full."

"I'll take care of that," said Mama, still angry. Lice were no laughing matter to her.

I expected Mama to produce her solution right then during bath time, but she did not. I did not learn what she had in mind until next morning when we were ready to go to the train. She produced a bonnet decorated with tucks and bows and fastened it securely under my chin, yanking and knotting the ties until I burst into tears. After Mama finished, Homer took me by the hand and led me out the back door and down the porch steps. We sat on the bottom step while he gently loosened and retied the bonnet so I could breathe more easily. He comforted me with soothing words and told me how much he hated the others for laughing and making remarks about me.

Papa appeared a few minutes later to tell us it was time to go. Before starting for the wagon, he held me close a moment and kissed me goodbye. Taking my brother's hand, he said, "It's up to you, son. Look after her and try to keep her out of your mothers way."

Homer squared his shoulders and seemed to grow. "I will, Papa. I'll take care of Ressie."

94

I was content and happy to be placed under my brother's protection.

The trip to town was not very enjoyable. Mama fretted the whole way over how Papa and the older girls would manage things without her for such a long time. Every few minutes, she would think of something else which might happen during her absence and give Papa instructions for how to deal with it. Our arrival at the station gave a new direction to her thoughts, and she busied herself making sure we were all presentable enough to make a favorable impression on anyone who might see us. Even I passed inspection in a new dress and my bonnet of organdy, lace and ribbons. We made quite a group on the station platform: Mama, Homer and I, our twin baby sister and brother, three trunks, and a fair amount of hand luggage, all bound for Georgia.

From the moment we boarded the train, the new smells were thrilling to me; coal soot, hot steam, sweat, spittoons, cigar smoke, stale food and dirty restrooms. I reveled in the smells and the excitement of sounds; hissing steam, chugging engines, babies crying, the clank of mail carts and squeak of luggage, "All aboard," called the conductor, and the step block hit the car platform.

We waved to Papa as the huge train strained itself to move. Goodbye - - goodbye - - goodbye. That was the sound of the steam and the wheels, faster and faster, until the sound became Grandma's - - Grandma's - - Grandma's. We were on our way. I watched the world run away from me as the train gathered speed.

When we first entered the coach, the windows were closed and flies swarmed everywhere. Several passengers opened their windows and got rid of the flies only to find themselves covered with cinders and black coal smoke. Either way the coach was hot. When the conductor came to take tickets, he noticed the sweat on my face and suggested that Mama remove my bonnet.

"We can't," I said, "Homer got lice from the Walker kids."

Mama could easily have thrown me from the coach. Instead, she pinched my arm until I cried out. My brother took my hand, and we moved to the end of the seat out of Mama's way. We were a source of amusement for passengers sitting near us for the rest of the trip.

It was not long before Homer and I discovered the toilet room, and it fascinated us. It was very different from the kind we had at home, and we investigated every corner. There was a mirror on the door but no wooden box of lime, and another omission puzzled me even more. I pulled Homer's sleeve.

"Where's the pages from the catalogue?"

"They ain't got none," said Homer. "But there's papers in that thing that work just as good."

We pulled several sheets from the dispenser, intrigued by the way extracting one brought the next into position. Half a dozen tissues gave us another excuse to flush the toilet. We pulled the long chain and watched the water splash out on the tracks, then stared through the hole at the racing procession of ties and cinders.

"We better get back." Homer said finally, with reluctance. "Mama'll wonder where we're at."

I nodded and turned to open the door. It would not budge. Homer joined me, but our combined efforts were still not enough to move the handle. Homer took out his penknife and pried at the bolt with no better success. My brother and I looked nervously at each other. We had managed to lock ourselves in, and Mama would not be pleased if she found out about it.

"Maybe if we pound on the door, somebody'll hear us and let us out," I suggested.

"Yea," agreed Homer. "Lets try."

We banged on the door with our fists, but the noise did not seem to attract any attention. At least, nobody came to learn the cause.

"Ain't no use," said Homer. "Train's making too much noise. We're going to have to yell."

Yell we did, and it got results, though not quite the ones we were hoping for. It was not just anybody passing by who heard us. It was Mama, and she could not get the door open either. She had to call the conductor to let us out, and by the time that was accomplished, she was quite ready to take her mortification out on us. As we stepped through the door, she grabbed each of us by an arm and dragged us back to our seat in the coach where we were spanked soundly in front of the other passengers. Mama picked each of us up bodily and set us down hard on the seat. "Now stay there!" she said, and meant it.

We did as we were told. However, our seat was next to the water and cup dispenser, another wonderful discovery. No matter how many people came to get drinks of water, there was always a fresh paper cup ready for use.

My brother wanted to see how the cup dispenser worked, so when Mama was dozing, he quietly removed it from the wall, using his penknife for a screwdriver. I watched every phase of the operation and helped where I could. I held the screws.

Just as Homer got the cup dispenser detached and lifted it down where we could look at the inside, the conductor appeared. He seemed huge, standing spraddle-legged in the aisle, scowling down at us. "Put it back - - exactly as you found it," he said and crossed his arms, waiting to see the order obeyed.

Homer put the cup dispenser back immediately, but in his hurry he forgot one of the screws. I was afraid of what might happen if the conductor saw there was a screw left over, and I did not want my brother to get in any more trouble, so I solved the problem as best I could. I swallowed the screw.

The commotion waked Mama, of course, and she was furious. She slapped me, confiscated Homer's penknife, and gave us each a scolding for good measure.

We sat quietly for a while after that, but the horsehair train seat got harder and harder, and we were bored with nothing to do. We felt around on the seat for the sharp end of the horse hairs and pulled out a number of them. They were long and black, and it was fun to pull them out, but we were afraid to take too many. Mama might catch us with them and give us another of her lickings.

For lack of a more interesting pastime, I watched the flies crawling on the window. One of them went straight up the glass, and as I followed it with my eyes, I noticed a silk cord which ran along the coach from one end to the other above the windows.

I tapped Homer on the shoulder. "What's that?" I whispered and pointed to the cord.

My brother shrugged. "I don't know. But it looks kinda like that thing at doctor Kelley's, the thing they pull when the maid comes."

"'Spose it's the same?"

"Might be. We can pull it and find out."

Homer stretched his hand toward the cord, but he was not quite tall enough to reach it. He looked around for something to use as a hook.

The seat just behind us was occupied by an old man, hard of hearing and partially blind, who was sleeping with his head against the window as he had been for most of the trip. His cane hung invitingly on the back of our seat. It was exactly long enough.

Taking the cane, Homer yanked the cord. With grinding metal and hiss of air, the train came to a sudden stop, throwing us against the back of the seat ahead, where Mama sat with the twins. Realizing instinctively that we were responsible, Homer hung the cane back where he got it and looked a warning at me. Instantly, we were "fast asleep."

We were not a minute too soon. For the conductor came at a dead run. After the episodes of the toilet and the cup dispenser, he had certain natural suspicions. While he stood in frowning anger trying to decide whether we were the culprits or not, we pretended the sudden stop had just awakened us. I took my cue from Homer's pressure on my arm and started bawling louder than the other children.

Awakened by the sudden stop without understanding it, the old fellow sitting behind us came to our rescue. He reached up and touched the conductor on the arm. "Where can a feller find a privy?" he asked in a quavering voice.

"So it was you!" the conductor stormed. Without answering the question, he delivered the lecture that had been intended for us, signaled the engineer and left the coach. Homer took the old man by the arm and showed him the restroom. We giggled afterward at our narrow escape.

When the train reached Birmingham, we had a layover before going on to Atlanta, and a few hours' span of time was never more welcome to Homer and me. We would have raced off the train the instant it stopped, but Mama had other ideas. She saw to it that we each had a piece of hand luggage.

Much to my embarrassment, I got the small chamber pot in a drawstring bag. It did not occur to me or Homer that few people would know what I carried unless I took it out and showed it to them. I felt that everyone was sure to recognize it at once as something shameful, so I ducked my head and held onto Homer's coat with one hand while I carried the evil-smelling pot in the other.

The conductor was not gentle in helping me down from the coach. As he lifted me from the top step, my hat came loose, and in trying to catch it, I hit him in the face with the pot. He uttered a startled, "Gawk?" and tossed me to the loose gravel where I lost my footing and fell. The pot made a loud enameled sound as it hit the ground.

Homer tried to help me but only succeeded in dropping the basket of lunch. Mama's patience had already been given too much to tolerate for one day. "Pick em up," she said between tight lips while trying to smile prettily at the conductor. "Pick em up and hurry!"

We clambered up a mountain of steps to the main terminal, swiping up dirt from everything we touched as we went. Inside, a constant whirr of activity put the fear of the unfamiliar in our hearts. People were everywhere, talking, humming and whistling for redcaps. Announcers yelled, and mothers scolded their crying children.

Mama led us through the confusion to the ladies waiting room, a huge high-ceilinged place with marble columns supporting the roof and a short mezzanine to the second floor. The sitting room was furnished with lounge chairs, rockers, leather-tufted lounges with built-in pillows, settees and here and there a desk with a straight chair. There were six or eight baby beds in a glassed-in enclosure for the benefit of those women traveling with children, and women with children filled the room. Mama had one bed for all of us smaller ones, but Homer and I were too excited to rest. We wanted to run and play and stretch our legs after the hours on the train.

We were having a game of tag around the marble columns, laughing with sheer relief, when a fat, bosomy woman sprawled in a lounge chair hollered to Mama, "Can't you keep them youn'uns quiet? I can't sleep in all that racket."

Mama promptly put us to bed, but we had not seen everything we wanted to see in the terminal. After a few minutes in bed, Homer nudged me, and I began to whimper. "Ssssip! I gotta go, Mama. I just gotta go."

Mama was disgusted, but she did not dare order me to stay in bed. She pointed out the general direction of the ladies' restroom and made Homer go with me to make sure I got to the right place, which is what we had hoped to accomplish. Homer was supposed to wait outside, but there was no one else in the restroom, and it was one of the most beautiful places I had ever seen, so I went back to the door and motioned my brother to come have a look.

There were mirrors everywhere, three whole walls of them, more than either of us had ever seen in one place before. We entertained ourselves with the mirrors for quite a while, making faces and twirling and sneaking up on the reflections. Then, we knew we would have to be getting back, or Mama would come to look for us.

Just as we were leaving a huge cockroach dashed out from a wall crack, and I scooped him up and handed him to Homer. I knew exactly what I wanted to do with that cockroach, and so did my brother. We snickered and grinned.

Since Homer had his hands full with the cockroach, he could not help me button my drawers, so I held them up going back to the waiting room. We tiptoed past Mama, who was sleeping somewhat peacefully in a lean-back lounge chair, and past the woman who'd had us sent to bed. She had removed her false teeth and was snoring with her mouth open. Her pink wrapper had come loose, exposing a perfect crevice. Homer looked at me, and I climbed into bed very quietly. He flipped the roach onto her bosom, and it, being an expert at finding niches to hide in, darted into the nearest one. Homer jumped into bed, and we were instantly "asleep."

The woman awakened with a start, screamed, yanked off her wrapper and corset and yelled for help. She shook the cockroach loose in the process. We watched it scuttle across the floor in search of a new hiding place as we sat up in bed rubbing our eyes and pretending her scream had wakened us.

Startled out of a doze, Mama was immediately solicitous of the woman's welfare. When she was settled, Mama explained she must have eaten something which disagreed with her and had a nightmare over it. "Try some pepsin," Mama urged. "I always carry it to settle the stomach. You never know when you'll get something tainted in one of these places."

Homer and I smiled at each other, satisfied. We'd had our revenge.

Mama finally allowed Homer and me to walk around if we were quiet, and we were. We did not want to be sent to bed again. When Mama saw how well we were obeying her, she even bought us a box of chums for a reward.

The waiting room and adjacent mezzanine held many features of interest for us. Smells told me the story, hot summer smells; dirty, tired humans, hot bales of cotton, steamy coal soot and engine grease, varied smells of poorly-prepared foods contrasted with the tantalizing aroma of hickory smoked ham, turnip greens and hot cornbread. I will never forget the pensive faces that lined the iron guarded platform and filled the waiting room, hopes, fears, longing, wistful desire and sad farewells. Each face was a story in itself.

Homer and I watched a young woman with her blind father. They occupied one end of a long wooden bench in the waiting room. The father, a user of chewing tobacco, had been directed to a spittoon, and we watched fascinated as he hit it with complete accuracy every time.

Spit-choo.

He chewed a while and seemed to relish the gob of brown juice worked up. Then, he aimed and let go. Remarkably, he hit the hole with only a minimum of splashing. On the floor between the old fellow and his daughter sat an oversized lunch basket from which the daughter had removed a banana. Talking with a full mouth and evident relish, she was recounting her troubles in loud and vehement tones.

"Mama couldn't bring him in to see Dr. Barker, and so I bring him. Has to spend the whole day fur a little while - - just a little while - - with the doctor, and he sez - - - ." Homer looked at me, and we walked up and stood close to the old fellow. I asked politely, "Can't you all see?"

"Nup," he replied. "Not no more. Got a catter-something-or other, ain't I, Rosie? What's that thing I done got?"

Happy for another audience, Rosie started her explanation over, but since we were only children, she directed the whole thing on the hapless woman sitting next to her on the bench, probably for the third or fourth time. Rosie was oblivious to everything but the story she was telling, and my brother was gradually able to switch the lunch basket and the spittoon. I sympathized with the old man, being careful to stay clear of the flecks of spittle that flew constantly

104

from his over-full mouth. When the switch was made, I patted his knee and said, "Bye now."

We skipped off to a safe distance and watched. Finishing her banana, Rosie turned to get fresh provisions, only to see a "kersplat" of tobacco juice hit the top of the lunch basket. The poor old man hardly knew what happened, but she had a very good idea. She looked around for us, but we had already ducked out of sight to avoid discovery.

Enjoying the comedy behind us, we went in search of other entertainment and found it on the outside mezzanine. Freight and express commodities stacked on handcarts emerged from the bowels of the terminal below, and we had a good look at all of it, for the carts had to go up a fairly steep ramp to reach the loading platform, and the men who pulled them could not climb the ramp very fast.

Goods came and went in seemingly endless variety, but one thing in particular attracted our attention, a casket with a glass top. We could look straight down from the mezzanine at the corpse of an old man with a long gray beard. The two black men pulling the dray were laughing and joking, and we watched them with interest, as did a small Negro boy standing at the foot of the ramp. He reminded us of Blue.

"Bet he'd like some of our chums," said Homer.

"Sure," I agreed.

A flight of stairs led from the mezzanine to the ground, and Homer started down them, but he tripped at the top, grabbed the iron rail to keep his balance, and the box of chums went flying. It thumped on top of the casket, bounced and hit one of the men pulling the dray, square between the shoulder blades. He let go the handle of the cart and ran, and his companion was only a few steps behind him, frightened at his friend's action even if he did not completely understand the reasons for it. The cart rolled back down the ramp and hit the wall, throwing open the lid of the casket. The boy whom we had intended to give some of our chums stared at it in horror for a moment, then ran after the two men.

It shook us up a little, too. We remembered everything Blue had told us about the results of fooling with the dead and our own experience with digging in the old cemetery. Besides, there was Mama, who might come to look for us at any minute. If she found out we had been involved in what happened, the lickings we had been given in the past would be nothing to the ones we would get this time. And this time we had not really done anything to deserve them.

We headed back for the ladies' waiting room in a hurry and met Mama just as she was coming out on the mezzanine. "What have you been doing?" she asked.

"Nuthin'," said Homer.

Mama looked skeptical. She took a few steps toward the edge of the mezzanine, but the announcer called the train for Atlanta just at the right moment. Mama hustled us back to the waiting room for a quick hand and face wash before boarding. Homer and I were happier to get back on the train than we had been to get off. Mama may have been surprised at our change of heart, but did not ask about it. We were relieved at that. If she had been in a different mood. We might have had a hard time coming up with a satisfactory answer.

Chapter IX

Grandpa's Magic Stone

The rest of the journey was something of a trial. We were all getting tired, and the food was becoming a little stale and monotonous. Mama's patience had worn thin along with her vanity. She had reached an emotional low ebb where a pinch and a slap followed all too quickly on the command, "Behave!" Knowing we had better watch our step now, Homer and I became cautious and quiet.

From Atlanta out to Lula where our grandparents lived, the train was not too crowded. There were enough vacant places that each of us got a seat to himself. At last we could stretch out and sleep.

It was mid-afternoon when the conductor, a cousin of ours from Savannah, helped us onto the rocky platform area at Lula. Coming toward us was a tall white-haired man in a dark suit, evidently

Grandpa from the way Mama smiled at him. He waved to the conductor, halloed greetings and continued talking in one breath.

"Well, Jeremiah, what you got here for me? Grandchildren, I'll be bound, I just imagine they've been a handful for you, Emma. You poor woman."

He gave Mama a hug which took in both her and the babies she was holding. At the state Mama had reached, all she needed to push her over the edge of tears was a sympathetic ear. She began to cry.

"Now, now, Emma." Grandpa patted her shoulder. "You're all here, and you're safe, and that's what's important. These three trunks yours? And the parcels? That's quite a bit. I don't think we can take all of it in one trip. I'll send one of the boys back for what we can't manage."

Grandpa started gathering up luggage and kids with smooth efficiency. Homer looked at me, and I knew instantly what he was thinking. We had better be careful of what we did around Grandpa. He was someone who would not be easy to fool.

Mama started a lively conversation as we walked over to the buggy, all about our trip from Arkansas. I did not hear one word of it. My eyes were fixed straight ahead at Grandpa's surrey. It was upholstered with red leather. The outside was painted a rich black, and the top was trimmed with beige fringe. The horse was sleek and well-groomed, and the harness shone with polish. It all looked beautiful to me.

Grandpa picked me up to put me in the buggy. As I often did with strangers, I wilted. My legs became like wet straw. My arms dangled, and I put a vacant look in my eyes, an expression which most people found distracting.

Grandpa did not seem disturbed by it, however. "This one's far too skinny, Emma," he said, bouncing me good-naturedly in the air. "Your mother and Harriet will soon take care of that. How are you, little one? You must be about worn out from this long trip. Now, you just sit right there in front on the floor, and hold on to the dashboard, Old Trotter will have us home in no time."

He set me down, and I folded. Mama looked at him, shaking her head. "That one's different," she said.

Grandpa was looking straight at me, so he probably caught the impish grin I darted at my brother. "They're all different, Emma," he said, and tapped the top of my head with the big end of the buggy whip.

When we were all settled and the parcels wedged in around us, Grandpa climbed into the driver's seat. At his command to Trotter, the buggy started with a jerk and a swirl of dust as the wheels ground in the gavel.

I watched Grandpa out of the corner of my eye as we drove along. I did not know much about him really, only a few things I had heard Mama say. He was a judge on circuit in Grant County, and he had built a church for the community on his own land with his own money. He even provided the minister. I thought he must be rich to do that, and have faith in God, too, the way Mama said he did. He looked likable.

We talked about one thing of interest or another all the way to Grandpa's house, and he was at the center of it. He made a little over the babies, who really were beautiful, asked Mama questions about how things were going in Arkansas and found ways to bring Homer and me into the conversation. He did not ignore me completely or make me feel as if he did not care. I began to perk up. This visit held promise.

The first sight we had of Grandpa's farm was the gristmill at the foot of the hill. A spring of cold water bubbled up there and formed a pond out of which flowed a steady stream, The mill sat straddled over this creek from which it drew its energy. A huge wooden wheel slowly turned, dipping and pouring water over its cupped shelves. The sound was restful to hear.

Grandpa's house sat on the hillside above the mill. A lane wound up to it through young trees. The house looked huge, with tall columns in front and a wide verandah. A milk-house and barn were visible behind. I could hardly wait to explore, and I knew Homer felt the same way. The place offered endless opportunities for children with active imaginations.

When we reached the house, Grandpa reined the horse to a stop. "Well, Emma," he said, "you're home again. Welcome. Your mother has made arrangements for all of you, so I'll let her take over from here. Ah, here she comes."

The moment I saw Grandma coming across the verandah to meet us, I could tell where Mama got her vain ways. There was nothing wrong with Grandma, at least none of the obvious things which often went "wrong" with old people. She was tall and straight, a little heavy and bosomy. Her hair shaded from white in front to dark reddish brown, and she had it wound into a neat figure eight on the back of her head. She wore a plain brown dress and a stiffly starched apron with two big pockets. She seemed to enclose all of us in one vast embrace, a welcome that truly made us feel at home. She talked as if we had always lived near her and were just now returning from a trip to town. I did not catch everything she said, but I heard the end.

"Now, Emma. You will."

That was enough for me. I was content. Sometimes Papa said, "Emma, you will." Then, things ran right for a long time.

Between bringing in our parcels and being introduced to our new relatives, Homer and I did not have much time to explode the farm that afternoon, much as we would have liked to. We got no further than the smokehouse and might not have gotten that far, only the cook needed some sweet potatoes. We offered to help her carry them to the kitchen, more from a desire to see what was in the smokehouse than from any wish to do anything that resembled chores.

Grandpa's smokehouse was filled with good things to eat. Fruit was heaped in baskets, and smoked meat wrapped in gunny sacks hung from the ceiling. I closed my eyes and took a deep breath to draw in all the delicious smells. One basket of apples was especially inviting, red and shiny. I asked Harriet about them as she handed me the sweet potatoes to hold.

"Ain't none of them fo' eating," warned the cook. "Them fo' seed. Yo' granddaddy picked them special." She shepherded us out of the smokehouse and closed the door.

Mama was looking for Homer and me when we got back to the house. Apparently, with the trip from Arkansas still fresh in her mind, she was going to be sure we did not get into mischief the first day we were at Grandpa's. She kept a watchful eye on us until suppertime.

It took a long table to accommodate all of us for supper. Aunt Fannie and Aunt Maggie, Mama's two sisters, had also come for a visit and brought some of their children, so we made quite a houseful. Supper was milk and mush sweetened with molasses. Grandpa served each of us from a tureen at the head of the table, a big bowl for each grownup, a smaller one for each child. After supper Grandpa led us in evening prayers, and we went upstairs to bed.

Upstairs at grandpa's was room after high-ceilinged room, each containing three or four beds. He and Grandma needed that much space when several of their children came to visit at the same time. This was part of Grandma's domain, and she managed it well, allotting rooms to each of her daughters according to the number of children they had along. Aunt Fannie had only one son with her, so she and her boy Oscar were given quarters with Mama and all of us. Homer shared the bed with Oscar and Aunt Fannie, it not being seemly to put boys and girls of the same age together. Since I was considered a little peculiar, I got the trundle bed which was placed behind a screen near the fireplace. Homer was happy for me. He knew how pleased I was at having a bed to myself where I could watch the fire and listen to the grownups talk.

After the rest of the children were asleep, Mama and Aunt Fannie talked long into the night with the fire for company. An added stick of wood would sparkle and crack igniting, and their conversation would take on color. Then, as the fire dwindled to glowing coals, their tales became secretive and subdued. What they said seemed to draw strength from the flames.

Listening behind the silk screen, I heard many interesting things which I noted in my mind to repeat to Homer. Aunt Maggie was having difficulties with her in-laws. That was why she had come to visit Grandma. Aunt Ethel had a retarded child, and Uncle Joe had lost his eyesight in a gun accident. When they had clucked and exclaimed enough over other people's troubles, Mama and Aunt Fannie got around to their own, and Mama told Aunt Fannie about me.

"Dr. Kelley says she's all right, Fannie, but I don't know. She is so different from the others. Seldom says a word. Seems to lose the ability to talk, then, I swear I'm dreaming it. She will say the most unexpected things. And at the very moment you least want her to. She and her brother brought lice home from school, so what does she do as soon as we get on the train for Birmingham? She tells the conductor all about it in a voice that carried up and down the train. I was so mortified, I could have dropped right through the floor of the coach. You know me, but those people didn't, and I'm sure they thought we lived in filth and dirt. I just don't understand her at all. I hope to get her to Dr. Edwards in Savannah while we're here. He is supposed to know a great deal about people, children especially. What do you think?"

Aunt Fannie poked the fire before answering. "I think she's smart enough, Emma. You don't have to talk to be smart. I was noticing her at supper, the way she watched every move anyone made. My Oscar seems to like her, and it's evident that your Homer does. I think you can trust the judgment of children that way. You know yourself how they'll just torment and devil one that's not right, I wouldn't worry about her."

After Mama and Aunt Fannie went to bed, I lay awake a long time, wondering if I really was different and what exactly that "different" meant. If it meant that a normal person ought to scrap and argue and fuss all the time the way my cousins did, I decided I would rather be the way I was. I liked being different from them.

By the time I had reached this decision, I was wide awake. The coals in the fireplace cracked every now and then, and there were other noises in the dark, not scary ones exactly but loud enough to keep me from going to sleep. By now it had been hours since supper, and I began to get hungry. I thought of the apples in Grandpa's smokehouse.

Soon, I heard Aunt Fannie snore and knew that she and Mama were asleep. I tip-toed out of bed and went downstairs. It was bright moonlight outside, so I had no trouble finding the smokehouse and opening the door. Inside, it was darker, but I knew about where the apples were and felt for them.

There were two baskets of fruit, as I remembered from the afternoon. The lower one was within easy reach, but the higher one, the seed apples, were much better. They were red and shiny and looked sweet. I knew it was wrong to take any of them, but

114

I was really tempted. I did not want the others. I finally made a compromise with myself. I would try to climb up and reach the seed apples. If I couldn't get up that high, I would take one of the others.

I pushed a brown-crock churn over to the table where the seed apples were. If I could balance on my knees at the edge of the table, I could reach the apples with no trouble. Using the churn for my ladder, I managed to get onto the table all right, but my foot slipped as I climbed up and the churn went over with a crash. Not only did the churn break, but it knocked over a barrel of apple-peeling beer and spilled that, too. I could tell what it was by the smell.

I paused in the dark until the echoes of the crash died away. After a minute or two, the barrel stopped gurgling also, and I knew the liquid inside had got down to the level of the bung hole. No more beer would trickle out, but by now my eyes were fairly accustomed to the dark and I could see that there was a sizable pool already on the floor of the smokehouse. I hoped no one found out that I was responsible.

Having done that much damage, I did not see where one seed apple more or less would make any difference. I took one from the basket and climbed back down. I was careful not to step in the spilled beer.

Leaving the door of the smokehouse unlatched, I went back to the kitchen and cut the apple in half. Half for Homer and half for me. I ate my half immediately, seed, core and peel. Then I crept upstairs to the room we all shared with Aunt Fannie and Oscar. I nudged Homer awake and shoved my present into his hand. The apple was

115

explanation enough of what I had been doing, and I knew he would eat every bit of it just as I had. There would be no evidence left for Grandpa or Mama to find.

Needless to say, Grandpa was furious next morning when he got a look at the smokehouse. After breakfast, he lined all of us children up outside and stood before us, dropping a smooth white stone from one hand to the other. His feet were firmly planted, and his face was stern, his eyebrows meeting in a frown. "Someone took some of the forbidden fruit," he said, and every child trembled at the words, especially me.

"Now," he continued, "I have here in my hand a magic stone. It knows which one of you opened the smokehouse last night, and it is going to tell me. When I toss this stone, it will hit the one who took the fruit."

I swallowed hard. I had not realized Grandpa knew magic. He blew on the stone, then it tossed high in the air over our heads. I ducked behind Homer.

"Ressie!" commanded Grandpa instantly. "Come here."

I walked toward him. There was nothing else I could do. I thought I was going to get a licking in front of all the rest, and I braced myself for it, but Grandpa sent them to do various chores. When the last of my cousins had gone to pick up sweet potatoes, he turned to me.

"What am I to do with you, little minx? Tell me, why did you take one of my seed apples, why not one of the others? Most children would have done that."

I looked him in the eyes and said, "I'm different."

"Huh," he snorted. "You look all right to me. What makes you different?"

I shrugged. "I just am. Mama says so."

Grandpa stood for a moment, gazing over the top of my head. His lips moved but no sound came. Finally, he seemed to each a decision. "Come with me," he said.

We went straight to the smokehouse, he holding my hand. He took two apples from the seed basket. "Take a good look at them, Ressie," he instructed. "A good look. Are they the same?"

I stared down at the apples. Each was round, red and shiny, but there were differences. One had a kind of bump near the stem. The other was perfectly round.

"They're different," I said.

Taking the apples from me, Grandpa returned them to the seed basket. Then he bent down and cupped my face in his hands.

"Every living thing is different, Ressie. Like those apples. People are the most different of all, even in our family. We all have two eyes, two hands and two feet, but inside we have different minds. We think differently. Our features, like those apples, are each a little different. Let's not feel we can do wrong things because people say we are different. All of us are different, but we still have to learn to do right. Understand?"

No one had ever told me that before, and it seemed when Grandpa said it I could understand. I knew from the way he looked at me that he was telling me what he believed was true, and was saying it because he cared about me.

"Yes, Grandpa," I said nodding. "I understand. I really do. Thank you."

He rested his hand on the top of my head. "Good, little minx," he said, and opened the door of the smokehouse.

I was out of there as fast as I could go. I ran to where the other children were picking up sweet potatoes. They met me with questions.

"What happened?"

"Did he beat you?"

"What'd he say?"

I refused to answer. I wanted to keep the things Grandpa had said to me for a secret. I could be that different from the others. I did not have to blab everything. And, for Grandpa, I would do right instead of wrong.

CHAPTER XI

Camp Meeting

Toward the beginning of August, talk at Grandpa's centered on the first camp meeting which would be held the last of August or the first of September, for two weeks. It was an expected part of the pattern made by the season, a kind of holiday with God's work in mind, after the crops had been laid by and before the harvest.

Although Grandpa lived only a short distance from the camp meeting grounds, we were to spend the whole time there, just like people who came from miles away. This meant many preparations, and we were all kept busy. Mama bought a 20-yard bolt of cloth, pink with red polka-dots and blue-green rings. She proceeded to make butterfly shifts for me, aprons for herself, shirts for Homer and pillow cases for straw pillows, all from that same material. Aunt Maggie did as much for her family, only she used blue checkered gingham which I thought was much prettier. One day I heard aunt

Maggie making the same point to Mama, and I stood outside the door to listen.

"I'm going to know mine as far as I can see 'em Margaret," said Mama in a matter-of-fact tone.

I had no trouble understanding what that meant. No matter how many people were at the camp meeting, Mama was going to keep her eye on Homer and me, and she was counting on the pink cotton to help her do it.

I was happy at my grandparents' and did not want to leave, especially not to go to any camp meeting. The way I had heard it described, it was one long church service from morning until night, and I had enough trouble sitting through the regular ones on Sunday. I wanted to stay home, but Mama had other ideas. When the day arrived for us to leave, she expounded them as she put a finishing touch to her packing.

"We _are_ going, and you _will_ behave. Hear me? Just perhaps, praying over is what you need. Anyway I'm going to request a special prayer meeting just for you. Maybe, just maybe, God will hear those prayers, and you can be a normal child."

I stared at the traveling Bible which sat on top of the ironed and mended clothes. "Grandpa said I could be different, 'cause that's the way God planned it. He said that, and I don't want any of' prayer meeting."

"See there! You're really defying God with your hateful ways."

Mama slammed the lid on the trunk full of clothes, took me forcibly by the arm and pushed me out into the long hall. She shoved me down on the bottom stair step and said, "You stay there and keep quiet 'til we are ready to leave."

Homer soon found me. Realizing my state of mind, he tried to relieve my fears. "Don't fret," he comforted. "I'll look out for you, just like I promised Papa."

"But you heard Mama and Aunt Maggie," I said mournfully. "We have to sleep in a straw bed with a squawking bunch of cousins, and I just know I'll get Birdie-May and Matilda-Rose. And they smell!"

Even Homer could think of no answer for that. He patted my shoulder and ran to help when Mama called him.

Our wagon was soon loaded and ready, quilts, blankets, food and clothes. We set off for Walnut Falls Church where the meeting was to be held. There were other people on the road heading for the meeting grounds also, in wagons and buggies, on horseback or on foot. When we arrived, I looked enviously at the covered wagons where some families were already setting up housekeeping. Other wagons had quilts or sheets hung around the sides to make a kind of private room underneath. It looked like it might be fun, to stay in a place like that, but nothing of the sort was for us. We went on to the community accommodations.

At one side of the meeting ground were three barracks-type buildings. They had a door in one end, a window in the other and bunk beds everywhere they could be fitted, three high along the walls and up to the window at the far end. Fresh straw, scrub cotton or cut up shucks were piled in the bunks for mattresses, each intended for as many children as could find room to sleep.

Mama, Aunt Fannie and a cousin with two squalling babies showed us our quarters. At the sight I was crestfallen and wept loudly. Mucus ran from my nose. I tried to look awful, and it had the desired result. The cousin asked for a place elsewhere so we were not too crowded. When the beds were arranged, Homer, Oscar and I went to have our first look at the camp meeting grounds.

Everywhere was bustle and confusion. Men were bringing in wood for the fires. Huge iron pots swung suspended from hooks and tripods. We watched a woman hang her willow basket of bread, pie and cookies from a tree limb, then wrap the limb with a rag soaked in kerosene to keep ants away.

A little further on, we had our first clear indication that camp meeting was a social occasion as well as a soul-searching affair. We heard the voice of one of Grandpa's neighbors from around the corner and stopped to listen.

"Now, Miz Harrison, I done taught Genora 'bout milking, cooking and canning, and she's real sweet to children, loves 'em, loves 'em. And she can sew a hem you cain't imagine. Course, she's not much fur looks, but as the saying goes, beauty's only skin deep. She'll be a fittin' wife for your Malcolm."

My eyes opened wider. "Is Genora Singer gonna get married right here at the camp meeting?"

"Shush, and you'll find out!" advised Oscar.

Above us, the wagon seat creaked as Mrs. Harrison shifted her weight. "Well, Miz Singer, I'll have to talk it over with Pa. Pa's got high hopes for our oldest. Course, he is shy and a bit leery of women folk, so I reckon it's no harm to give him some encouragement. We'll just have to bring them two together and see what's gonna be."

"That's right," agreed Genora's mother. "Some things just have to be left up to the Lord. Well, I got to get back to the wagon and finish shaking the dust out of my quilts, but when I saw you all drive up, I just had to tell you what was in my mind. I'll see you at the service."

As Mrs. Singer walked off in one direction, Homer, Oscar and I scampered away in another. In the shade of an oak tree, we stopped to pool our information and discovered we did not know as much as we would have liked. Genora Singer had been to church several times, but Malcolm Harrison was a complete unknown. We would have to wait for the service to have a look at him. Meanwhile, we still had a good half the meeting grounds to explore. We made the road our next objective.

A cloud of dust hung over the entrance to the camp meeting grounds from a steady stream of horses, mules and vehicles. Wagon after wagon arrived, many loaded with food. Grandpa had contributed meal, flour and oatmeal, straw, cotton and a young beef. Other farmers of the area were also generous, hauling in whatever produce was available, apples, peaches, cantaloupes, smoked meat, watermelons and chickens in coops. Nobody was going hungry at the camp meeting.

People were not the only ones in attendance. Flies swarmed, bees, yellow jackets and dirt daubers were all there to praise God and get saved. Gray squirrels and blue jays carried on their own form of preaching, squawking at the human invasion of their domain.

The noise was unbelievable to Homer and me. Women scolded and dogs barked. Roosters crowed, babies cried, children argued and fought. Suddenly, the church bell rang, cutting through the other sounds and silencing hem. Children and dogs were brought to heel, and the crowd started moving toward the brush arbor where services would be held.

Whenever possible, growing trees formed the supports of the arbor. A roof of brush and boughs provided shade and protection from unexpected rains which might otherwise cause a great deal of discomfort. The benches were boards laid between parallel logs. Only those intended for old people or women with suckling babies had backrests. Some people brought their own cane rockers to be assured of a comfortable seat.

Mama was waiting for Homer, Oscar and me when we reached the arbor. She pointed out seats for us on one of the benches. When I did not move fast enough to suit her, she pulled me by the skirt of the pink shift and sat me down where she wanted. Within the first few minuets, I knew that sitting on that board for hours of preaching would be penance enough for anything I had done wrong, even counting from way back.

People were crowding into the seats under the brush arbor now. Oscar punched me in the ribs. "There's the Singers." he whispered.

Genora Singer was as homely as I remembered her, with buck teeth and stringy brown hair, and if the boy Mrs. Singer had in tow was Malcolm Harrison, he was not much for looks either. His ears stuck out, and he was skinny as a rail. I would have liked to see how Mrs. Harrison's "encouragement" worked out, but I did not get the chance. They sat on the far side from us, and the benches between filled rapidly. Finally, everybody found seats. The ministers gathered on the platform around the altar, and the camp meeting was in progress.

Whether plans had been made in advance or whether the Lord stood among those present, everything seemed to fall into place. Brother Rorry held up his arms and said in a deep bass voice, "We are gathered together in the presence of God! Let us conduct ourselves accordingly."

I looked around at the bowed heads, then up at the heavens. Shining between the oak leaves, I thought I beheld the face of God. It was right over the arbor, and I could scarcely stand to look. I nudged Homer. He looked up and quickly bowed his head. I did the same, for I was a little ashamed of some of the things I had done at Grandpas'. I decided right then I had better behave from here on. Afterward, Mama said the prayer meeting did me a lot of good, but it was all because I saw God peeking at me through the roof of the brush arbor.

After that first evening, the camp meeting settled into its own kind of routine. The first service began at eight o'clock in the morning with prayers being offered for the women who had been appointed to do the cooking for the day and the people who would keep the fires burning. From there, the preachers relayed each other throughout the day. As soon as one talked himself hoarse, another took over. The sermons were simple for the most part, carrying a message everyone could understand. Over and over, we heard that a mans' word was something not to be taken lightly, that a good name for truth and honesty were a man's best assets, and that sharing freely with a neighbor was the greatest gift next to a man giving his life to God. The ministers were, for the most part, dedicated Christian men who sincerely hoped to see their congregation accept God and the Savior. They also showed an obvious partiality to their own way of thinking, Methodist, Baptist, or whatever, but no one seemed to mind.

I listened to the sermons which interested me and daydreamed through the others, just as I did at home. From the expressions I saw on the faces around me, I knew I was not the only one who stopped listening when the preaching got dull. Men sat leaning against trees or sprawled on the ground. Children nodded off from boredom and slept fitfully leaning on anyone or anything within reach. Such behavior was evidently expected, for there were tow sacks filled with cotton, straw or shucks which could be used as pallets.

Homer, Oscar and I soon learned that if we were quiet about things we did not have to sit through all the preaching. In fact, when Mama was with the relations, she often preferred to have me somewhere else, for she never knew what tasty bit of gossip I might have overheard about the people she was with. She would make an excuse for us to leave, and we would be off before she could change her mind.

We observed the courtship of Malcolm Harrison and Genora Singer with interest. It took place right out in the open, so there was no trouble about seeing what went on. Malcolm walked Genora back to the Singer wagon every evening after vespers. Both had been brought up to obey their parents, so when they found out they were supposed to like each other, they did their best to fall in with the idea.

Either Mrs. Harrison or Mrs. Singer was always finding some way to bring the young people together. It was plain each woman was eager to get her offspring married and off her hands. Each worked hard to make her shy, homely child into someone desirable. The best the Harrison's had was reserved for Malcolm, starched shirts, pressed pants, shined shoes and hair grease. The Singers did the same for Genora. She got the lace and ribbons, red cherry stain for the lips and crushed honeysuckle or wild rose petals in her clothes.

Pretending we were "that age," Homer, Oscar and I chose and discarded any number of available boys or girls as marriage partners. I began to make secret plans for my own wedding at some future time, but my plans always stuck fast on one obstacle. I could not imagine Mama ever making over me the way Mrs. Singer did over Genora. It was almost enough to make me wish I had buck teeth.

When we got tired of watching people, Homer, Oscar and I went exploring. On one of these excursions, we crossed the forbidden creek at the back of the tent grounds. In the distance, a red barn and farmhouse were visible, and we wandered aimlessly toward the house, as we walked, we heard the plaintive meow of a kitten. We soon located it among the weeds, and Homer put it in the bosom of his shirt. It was scrawny and hungry, and we ran back for the housing sheds to find it some food.

Kittens or cats were forbidden on the camp meeting grounds because of their natural effect on hound dogs. Most of the men had brought dogs and went rabbit hunting between services to pass the time and provide fresh meat. We knew what would happen if the kitten got away, so while Homer went to find food for it, Oscar and I made it a hiding place in the dirty linen. We had good intentions. At the first opportunity, we planned to take it to the barn at Grandpa's where it would find plenty to eat. Milk was always provided for the barn cats there.

The last thing before vesper services, we checked on our kitten to make sure it was safe and fed. It was sleeping among the clothes, so we tucked the dirty linen back around it and went to the brush arbor.

Vesper services began at twilight. A fire on either side of the arbor helped provide light. Lanterns hung on the posts completed the illumination, but there was still not enough to interfere with the sleep of anyone so inclined. The minister for that evening preached a three-hour sermon through which many of the congregation slept. Finally, he sent a call to the altar. "Praise ye the Lord," his voice boomed. Everyone including the children jerked awake.

"Let every living thing praise the lord!"

"Meow, meow," came a piteous cry from the rear of the arbor, where praising the Lord or not nobody could say. At the sound, every dog on the grounds was alerted, and they came on the run, barking, baying and sniffing. Homer and I saw a flash of gray fur as our scrawny kitten went streaking down the aisle toward the platform with a half dozen hounds in pursuit.

"Ring!"

"Brownie!"

It was futile to call off the dogs. The temptation was too great. But the owners tried.

"Tall Boy!"

"Delfeaser!"

Men scrambled up onto the platform to get their dogs. The minister fell over the water keg in his haste to get out of the way. Our kitten climbed a pole to the roof of the bush arbor, and the dogs circled the pole, barking and wagging their tails, happy to have treed their quarry. Awakened by the excitement, babies cried, people hollered and one elder sitting at the side kept yelling, "Praise the Lord!" "Praise the Lord!"

Homer and I laughed so hard at the cat that was "saved" that we were afraid Mama might suspect we had something to do with what had happened, but apparently she did not. At least she did not ask the congregation to pray over us, the usual fate of children who misbehaved at the camp meeting.

Grandma laughed over the incident as hard as we did. She said she had not seen anything so funny for a long time. That made us feel better. We decided we had not committed such a terrible sin after all.

We never found the cat again, and it was probably just as well for us. We developed quite a reputation as it was, and our clothes helped identify Homer and me. Mama was right in thinking red polka-dots on a pink background would stand out in a crowd. "I saw them pink dotted children," was a denunciation we often heard, or if the blame had to be shared. "There was a checkered child in with them dotted ones." We became so well known that we could walk

129

up perfectly innocent of wrong doing and be ordered away. "Gwan! You dotted children ain't nothing but trouble. Your ma needs to put your names in for constant prayer."

Actually, there was too much going on at the camp meeting for us to make a really noticeable disturbance. Between sermons, there was singing, both of hymns and secular music, and people participated whether they could really sing or whether they only thought they could. There were games of horseshoes, hopscotch, ball and marbles. Women mended or did handwork while they caught up on the doings of neighbors and relations. There were fights and arguments, especially among us children, but those were usually settled without resort to adult intervention. No child wanted the humiliation of having his name called for prayer in the meeting.

There was always plenty to eat. People who felt themselves better off than the general run had their own kettles, fires and meals apart from the "riffraff." They made a great display of giving leftovers to the main table. Many people were too proud to touch this offering, but not Homer and I. We enjoyed the variety. It was good food, and Mama did not spend too much time trying to keep us from sampling it. "They're just children. You know how children are," she would say, thus establishing in a delicate way that she was not accepting charity and not in need of any either.

For the most part, the people at the camp meeting were poor but they kept clean to the best of their ability. Large churns of lye soap with gourd dippers were provided by different people for those without. Nothing was said about conserving the soap, but it was used sparingly. Everybody seemed to understand that it was a commodity hard to come by. Women wore long dresses and underskirts, and where there were children, these garments were often used as wash cloths, hand towels and hankies. Water for washing came from the creek.

With so many people gathered in one place, the privies were never <u>not</u> in use. Men often avoided the problem by simply going to the woods, but that was not as easy for women to do. There was always someone in the women's, a hastily constructed thing made of poles. It was covered on three sides, and the open side had two good-sized logs placed side by side over a deep ditch. In spite of the fact that this seat was scrubbed daily with lye soap and water, one usually came away from it smelling of urine and feces. A barrel of lime sat in one corner, and a shingle whittled into a paddle was used to dip lime over the days' deposit. This was supposed to cut the smell and discourage flies. It failed miserably.

Possibly because of these unhygienic conditions, the camp meeting was a natural breeding place for disease. One barracks of children came down with measles. Dr. Crawford was attending the meeting, and he quarantined the children which made an added burden for some of the women. Homer and I had had measles, so we were allowed a freedom other children were forbidden. Between the prayers of the congregation and Dr. Crawford, the disease ran its' course in a short time and everyone recovered.

None of these discomforts or inconveniences dampened the spirits of people at the camp meeting. A holiday mood prevailed, one well suited to such events as the wedding of Genora Singer and Malcolm Harrison. It was not a surprise, of course, but when Brother

Rorry announced that it would take place at midmorning service the following day, that made it official, and everyone pitched in to help with the preparations.

Since Grandpa's was about the closest house, Grandma and Aunt Alice went home to bake the wedding cake. Other women put heads and belongings together and came up with a pair of black laced high-top shoes and a white dress for Genora. "I brought this dress to be baptized in," ventured Sarah Merthyn hesitantly, "But if'n your Genora wants to wear it, I think it'd look real pretty on her." Mrs. Singer accepted the offer at once. She and Mrs. Merthyn were up half the night altering the dress to fit and probably giving Genora some advice about what she ought to expect as a married woman.

Nothing happened to interfere with the wedding. There was a shower of rain in the early morning, just enough to leave the air fresh and clean, but it stopped before the service. Malcolm and Genora stood up in front of the congregation kind of timid about the whole thing, as Homer, Oscar and I could plainly tell from our seats up toward the front. They acted like they were scared to look down and scared to look up, like they wanted to touch each other but were not really sure that it was all right. When Brother Rorry said they were man and wife, all the men at the service shouted and tossed their hats in the air.

Lunch was scrumptious right down to the last crumb of the wedding cake, and there was singing afterward, but the real fun came that night when the whole camp meeting shivareed Malcolm and Genora. To get their honeymoon off to a good start, the new Mr. And Mrs. Harrison were escorted to the Singer wagon with whooping and hollering and beating on pans. The commotion set every hound dog on the grounds to baying and howling, adding considerably to the noise, The newlyweds got the curtained-off "Room" under the Singer wagon, Mr. and Mrs. Singer moving their mattress and quilts up into the wagon bed. Some of the men joked about Malcolm Harrison starting off his married life so close to his mother-in-law. It took a long time for the camp to settle down, which was fine with Homer, Oscar and me. For once, we got to make as much noise as we wanted without anyone trying to shush us.

The wedding of Malcolm and Genora encouraged several other couples to tie the knot, and no one was more at the center of the resulting bustle than Sarah Merthyn. Her baptizing dress was tucked in, let out, spliced, lengthened and shortened to fit several brides. It served nicely for those unable to provide a white dress of their own.

For one reason or another, the camp meeting was memorable to everybody, but perhaps the people who had the most to show for it were the moonshiners. Corn liquor was a must for every social gathering, and the meeting was no exception. The men in attendance made frequent trips to the wagon yard for fellowship meetings, and they were always in a more receptive mood at the next service.

When Homer, Oscar and I wandered that way, we were met with good-humored laughter. The men tossed us in the air and boosted us from hand to hand. The smell on their breath was one I could not mistake. I remembered the jug of Uncle Sam's home brew we had found in the orchard.

The Thompson boys, who operated a still, must have made a handsome sum before the end of the camp meeting. Whether real or all for effect, the ugliest and most brutal looking of the Thompsons was saved, and the minister used him as an example of what God could accomplish. Everybody was eager to see him baptized.

The baptismal was set for the last day of camp meeting, a Sunday. Since in a sense it was the high point of the whole meeting, everything possible was done beforehand to clean up the grounds and get ready to leave. Wagons were loaded and dogs tied to the wheels so they could not run off at the last minute. Hay, straw and shucks were cleared and burned at a big bonfire at the early morning service. The smell was offensive, since many children wet the bed and the mess was further saturated with the odors of vomit, measles, sex and sweat. Everybody stood upwind, tossing in discards of one thing or another they did not want to carry home.

After cleaning the grounds, we had lunch, then got ready for the baptismal service. Walnut River which flowed back of the church, had been chosen for the baptizing. Its banks were lush with vines and bushes. Hidden here and there was a moss-covered rotting log. Wild grape vines, buzzing with flies and yellow-jackets, hung in clusters over the river, giving a horn-of-plenty look. Goldenrod, elderberry leaves and cowslip formed an altar of natural beauty, and the water churned into froth at the small waterfall above the site.

The baptismal was a very emotional time. Men and women were lined up along the shore solemn and weepy. Many of those who had hesitated now wished they had professed Christ openly.

Along with other children, Homer, Oscar and I had perched on the large, low-hanging limb of a maple tree. I had a lard pail of acorns with me, huge, brown and smooth. They were the loveliest part of the whole meeting to me, and we children used them among ourselves as money. On the present occasion, we laid bets on who would do the most shouting when they were immersed.

The baptismal went along fairly uneventfully until it came the turn of Mrs. Mueller. It had taken much urging, talking, and prayer to "bring her across." She was a tremendous, heavy woman, and when she waddled up to the minister on the bank, one could see she wore little except a large Mother Hubbard nightgown. She grasped the minister's hand and he finally maneuvered her into the water deep enough.

He had some misgivings - - written all over his face - - but he knew his duty. He supported Mrs. Mueller on one side, and his assistant did the same on the other, trying to find secure footing all the while. She was depending on them to save her if anything went wrong.

I laid all my acorns on my brother's. He was betting five to one the minister would drop her.

Sure enough!

The minister must have stepped on a rock or into a hole. He and Mrs. Mueller both went under, grabbing, rolling and tumbling. The assistant looked wildly around, then started for the shore, hollering, "Save 'em, Lord! Save 'em!"

Homer promptly collected acorns from all the children who had faith in the minister.

Several men waded out in their Sunday clothes, and finally, a semblance of order was restored. Mrs. Mueller stood on the bank after her ordeal, a real treat for some eyes. Her white gown was sculptured to every part of her enormous frame. When we played at baptizing afterward, it was always these characters we chose to imitate.

As evening shadows began to deepen, people shook hands, prayed together, wept together, then one by one, reluctantly left. Children who had made friends waved to each other as far as they could see. As Mrs. Singer watched her daughter leave with the Harrisons, I saw on her face the calm, satisfied expression of a woman who had accomplished her purpose.

Since the distance to Grandpa's was short, we were among the last to leave, Grandpa had promised that he and his family would finish the cleanup job when everybody else was gone. It meant no shirking for anyone, for there was a lot that needed to be done.

It took a team of horses to drag the heavy iron pots into the protection of a lean-to. Iron tripods and pulleys were also stored there, along with the many items people had forgotten, enamel pitchers, wooden spoons, irons, tin pie plates, a single-tree, a jacket, a hubcap. All were carefully placed in a wooden box to be returned at the next camp meeting, or earlier if possible. They were perfectly safe, no one would have thought of stealing them.

During the cleanup, Homer and I found a silver dollar. We hid it first one place then another, until Oscar discovered what we had. "Halves or else," he said, looking meaningfully in Grandpa's direction.

Homer was willing, but money was something with which we had had very little experience. It was hard to figure out how to share without disclosure. After much thought, I make up my mind.

"It's God's money. I saw him looking straight down during the service."

"You just don't wanta share," accused Oscar.

I protested my innocence. "Course I do, but if you take money from God, the whole world may just collapse."

"She's right," agreed Homer, stopped short by the thought. "Ain't no ol' devil gonna take me to hell and burn me for no ol' money."

Oscar was swayed by this reasoning, but reluctantly. "How you gonna give it back?" he demanded. He was a good friend but also a stickler for detail.

"Give it to me. I'll show you. Come on."

I led the way to the river and stopped on the bank above the pool where the baptizing had been done. I pointed to the rippling water. "The minister said that when we were here, we were gathered to gather in the sight of God, so if we throw the dollar back in there, God'll see us, and he'll know we've done right."

Homer felt relieved to be free from the responsibility for the dollar. "I call that good thinking," he said.

"Me too, I guess," said Oscar, "but you better say some Bible words, it's fittin'."

I stood solemnly on the bank holding the coin. I thought of home back in Arkansas and Blue and his easy access to rhyme. "Kin you sweet talk God?" I asked.

"Sure." Homer nodded. "God knows just what you're gonna ask. He knows our problem, go on."

I took a deep breath. "Dear God, we stand on the bank with your money. We're giving it back to you, God Honey."

I tossed the coin into the middle of the stream, just below the water fall. It sank, drifting slowly to the rhythm of the flow, gleaming from the reflection of the sun. It was almost like the day I had seem God looking down at me through the arbor. I squinted up at the face of the sun, blinded by its brilliance. "You saw us, God." I said. "We give it back."

"Amen," said Homer, and Oscar followed his example.

We turned and walked back to the church where Grandpa was waiting for us. The camp meeting was over, and we were ready to go home.

CHAPTER XII

Right or Wrong - - Mama Style

Shortly after the camp meeting, Mama decided either that Georgia had had enough of us by now or that Arkansas could not get along without us any longer. Either way, she shepherded us through a round of goodbye visits, packed our clothes back in the three trunks, and got us on the train for the return trip. The last we saw of Grandpa, he was standing on the platform and we waved to him until the train rounded a curve and the station was out of sight.

The trip back to Arkansas was not as exciting as the trip to Georgia had been. Homer and I were old hands at rail travel, familiar with the flush toilet, the cup dispenser and the emergency brake, there was nothing else to discover. After a day and a half in the stuffy swaying coach, we were glad to hear that we had reached Arkansas, though we still had a long way to go to our destination.

Homer and I must have fallen asleep, for the next thing I knew, Mama was shaking us rudely awake. "Get up," she ordered. "We're almost there," when she saw our eyes were open, she began to gather up our belongings, pushing and stuffing.

I tried to get away before she remembered what I had been assigned to carry, but she thrust the chamber pot bag into my unwilling hands before I could escape. I looked at it in utter disgust.

The conductor brought a porter to help Mama get baggage and children disembarked. His duty performed, he disappeared on down the train with a sigh of relief and a shake of the head. I admit we were not much to look at. With soiled clothes and coal dust smudges around our eyes, we seemed to be made up for a minstrel show. Homer and I did not care. We pressed our noses against the dirty window to get the first glimpse of Papa.

The train whistled for a crossing and began to slow coming into the station. Wisps of steam floated past the window. Then, the platform came in sight, and we saw a familiar face.

"There he is!" I squealed. "There's Papa."

As I jumped down from the window, the enamel chamber pot in its muslin bag hit a brass spittoon, nearly spilling the contents. Mama glared at Homer as though it were his fault. "Get the child to the door and be quick about it," she said.

The train stopped with a jerk, throwing us in all directions. I dashed to the door and almost went over the bannister of the platform in my haste to get out. "Papa!" I yelled. "We're here! We're home!"

One by one, Papa lifted us down to the ground, planting a kiss on each small smudged face. "Here's my boy," he said to Homer. "And I see you've taken good care of Ressie."

Homer straightened with pride. He did not often hear words of praise. "Thank you, sir. I tried real hard."

Mama came down the steps and literally dropped into Papa's arms. He lifted her and the babies and swung them around. "It's good to have you back, Emma," he said.

Bag, baggage and chamber pot, Papa gathered us and our belongings and drove us home.

It felt good to be back at our own house, even though there were a thousand things to do. The older girls who had remained at home with Papa were more than willing to turn the management of the house back to Mama, and she in turn saw to it that Homer and I got our old jobs. Homer split the wood and I brought it in for the cook stove just like before, and Mama found a new chore for us as soon as she saw we were in danger of finishing the one already assigned.

When Blue showed up to welcome us home, Mama found chores for him too, but he did not seem to mind. We were happy to see him again, we told him what we had seen and done at Grandpa's, and he told us about everything that had happened while we were gone. Blue also knew songs to accompany every kind of work, so altogether, it made the chores go quicker.

We had not been home long before Mama discovered that her chickens had been dying of cholera, and she decided to clean the chicken house. It was a major undertaking. The word "clean" meant more to Mama than to most people.

Hot water was the first requirement. Homer and I filled the cast-iron wash pot with water from the well. Then, Mama sent us to the woods for pine knots, the resiny knots left on the ground after the rest of the pine tree had decayed and gone. We brought back tow sacks full for the fire. They burned long and furiously.

When the water was hot, Mama and the older girls set to work scrubbing the roosts, walls and windows with boiling water and lye soap. Homer and I were put to work with a number three wash tub and small fireplace shovels. We scooped the droppings from the sick chickens into the wash tub and hauled it to the garden where we dumped the loads about three feet apart to be spread out later and plowed under.

The smell was terrible, but we made the best of it. We had to under Mama's watchful eye. We pretended each tubful was a dead person, and with sighs, much nose holding and giggling, we carried out our share of the chore. Blue joined us, and the task almost became fun.

Our chickens were not bred fowls. They were hatched, usually out of the settings of eggs from the neighbors' chickens, and in those cases the mother-hen was always named in honor of the neighbor, Mrs. Tatum, Mrs. Payne, or whomever. As the chickens grew, they often acquired names of their own, given for some unusual coloring or distinctive characteristic. In this way, a chick that grew up to be a setting hen had both a first name and a last name.

Mrs. Marigold Wheeler was one of our most distinctive hens. Most of her tail feathers were missing, leaving a bare rear end, but it was her comb which caught the eye and inspired her name. It looked like a marigold flower that had been frostbitten but was determined to stay in blossom.

When Homer, Blue and I sat down for a breather, we saw Mrs. Marigold Wheeler scratching nearby, and the sight sparked an idea in Homer. "Know what?" he said. "We ought to make that ol' hen a sacrifice."

"How you figure that?" asked Blue.

I did not know exactly what my brother had in mind either, but I would never have admitted it openly the way Blue did. I just looked puzzled.

"You know," persisted Homer. "Preacher's always talking about it and reading about it from the Bible. When people wanted things to go right, they made a sacrifice, and we sure want this job to go right, cleaning the chicken house, don't we? I know I don't want to have it to do over."

Blue nodded doubtfully, and I seconded his agreement. I was always ready to follow where Homer led.

We waited and watched until Mama had gone to the house on an errand. Then Homer caught Mrs. Wheeler and carried her over to the wash pot, where he said a few words appropriate to the occasion, christening her at the same time.

"Mrs. Marigold Wheeler, we offer you as a sacrifice for all our hard work," he announced in a solemn voice, and calmly tossed her into the pot of boiling water. She squawked once as she dived to the bottom, and the deed was done. Blue and Homer used forked sticks and removed her quickly. We buried her under the next load of chicken droppings we carried to the garden. In our secret, we forgot how tired we were and got on with our job quickly.

When Mama returned from the house, she smelled the funny odor from the pot of boiling water, but it did not occur to her to connect it with the chickens. "Men!" she muttered. "They need someone to look after them. The water has probably smelled like that for a month, and William never noticed it. I'll have to get him to clean the well."

Walking on down to the chicken house, Mama noticed that Mrs. Wheeler was missing, but fortunately for us, the truth did not dawn on her even then. Marigold had not been one of her best layers, and she dismissed her absence with a shrug. "Maybe she's wandered off." said Mama. "She always was a strange one. Always neglected her chicks."

Homer, Blue and I were convulsed with laughter, but this did not arouse suspicion, as we had been giggling all along. We could not afford to let our secret come out. It would have been lickings all around if Mama had known the truth.

When Mama had scrubbed the roosts with the help of the girls, each log was clean and shiny. She then built a fire for smudge in an old can, green pine boughs and green hickory with pine knots to keep them burning. This smoke was kept going until the chicken house was a pleasant place to stand in and smell.

Mrs. Payne, Mrs. Steel, Mrs. Racker and Mrs. Tatum all left us before the cholera epidemic was over. We gave each of them a

Christian burial. We said a prayer, put acorns, moss and pretty stones on their graves. That made us feel we had made up for sacrificing Mrs. Marigold Wheeler.

Mama cleaned the chicken house so thoroughly that she wore out most of our brushes, which gave Papa some extra work to do. Papa made the brushes at our house. He worked at them in winter and on very rainy days. He sawed boards of oak in various lengths and widths, two of the same size for each brush. Holes were cut in one board to receive previously cut and twisted corn husks which formed the bristles. To finish the brush, the top board was fastened into place and held securely with iron clamps. A handle was screwed into a center hole to form a mop. Smaller brushes were made minus the handle.

Soap making was a job that got the whole family busy, and it had to be done, too, for the chicken house cleaning had done the same for our supply of soap that it had done for brushes. By the time Mama got the roosts and walls in a condition that satisfied her, our soap was running low.

Some of the preparations for soap making went on all year round. Out in the back wood lot, we had a small shed in which receptacles for scrap meat were kept. These consisted of four huge crock jars resting on a wheeled framework. The scraps got rank in short order, so when Homer and I were sent to take fat meat scraps to the soap shed, we made a game of it. We would take a deep breath, dash in and deposit the scraps, dash back out, fasten the latch and run for dear life before we breathed again.

The ash hopper was also a permanent feature in our yard. It looked something like an inverted house top. Into this, the ashes from three fireplaces and one cook stove were dumped as they accumulated. When it rained, the water trickled through the ashes leaving a lye deposit that would dissolve an angle worm in a matter of seconds. Homer and I knew it would. We had tried it.

On soap-making day all hands in the family were kept busy. The men removed the detachable front from the soap shed, hitched the mules to the wheeled cart and hauled the cart back with its empty containers and put the team away.

Mama, Homer, I and one of the older girls carried pails of lye water from the ash hopper and poured the water equally into the three pots. When the lye water, plus one can of store-bought lye, had been added to the fat, we began to stir, holding our noses to keep out the stink. It was an awful task.

When the mixture was well stirred, pine knot fires were lighted around the pots. The transformation was miraculous. The lye ate the meat, and as it was consumed, the smell changed. Until at last we had two small ten-gallon crocks of rich soap which would clean just about anything.

One jar was left at the wash place in a protected area. The other was taken to the house and set on the back porch. A small gourd dipper hung on the side of the jar for dipping the syrupy soap. A little went a long way.

Face and hand soap was made separately with good drippings and an added touch of rose water and glycerine. Only store-bought lye was used. The hard soap came from the pot boiling hot and was poured into a square wooden trough. Just before it hardened, Mama cut it into family-sized squares. It was used carefully and never left in a wet dish. The smell was rich and clean.

When Mama got her crock jars full of soap and her chickens cured of cholera, she felt that order had been restored in her domain and she could relax a little. She did not realize that another enemy had crept in despite her vigilance. It happened this way.

Our older brother Charlie acquired sudden wealth, two dollars earned at the cotton gin. When the carnival came to town, Papa allowed Charlie to go with his friends, provided he took Homer along. They returned with many wonderful prizes and purchases; a china slipper made into a pin cushion, an iron horse, a glass vase, a net bag containing all sizes of marbles and a pack of celluloid playing cards.

Charlie did not personally see anything wrong with cards, but he had sense enough to know that Mama might feel differently about them. Until he could feel her out on the subject, he hid the cards and other treasures in the cotton house, a shed we had to hold picked cotton until there was enough to make a bale. He was sure his things would be safe there.

In order to learn Mama's opinion without danger to himself, Charlie talked one of his friends into bringing a pack of cards over to our house. They sat on the edge of the porch shuffling the cards and fooling with them until Mama came out to see what was going on. Charlie found out what she thought right away. She pounced on the Lawton boy.

"Just what do you think you're doing, young man, bringing cards into this house? Cards are a tool of the devil, and don't you forget it!"

"But, Ma," protested Charlie.

"No buts about it." Mama was not to be distracted from her objective. She never took her eyes off Sid Lawton. "Boy, if that is your deck of cards, you put them back in your pocket and take them home. My children are not to have them. A respectable widow woman like your mother is, I'm surprised she lets you have them. If she knows you've got them."

Mama glared fiercely at the poor Lawton boy, as though to make him feel he had committed some dreadful sin. He gathered up his cards hastily and edged toward the gate saying, "Yes Miz Crenshaw. Like you say, Miz Crenshaw. You all come by sometime." Once out the gate, he fairly flew up the road.

The incident made it clear to Charlie that he would have to keep his own cards in the cotton house, and he did. It was a natural place, for we all played there. We could lay back in utter comfort against the soft cotton and exchange confidences. If we were quiet, Mama could pass close by looking for us and never know we were there. The cotton dulled sound.

One day in the cotton house, Charlie was showing us how to play a card game the Lawton boys had taught him. I cared nothing for numbers, so while the others played, my younger sister and I dug caves in the cotton and buried ourselves. I had just settled mown for a pleasant afternoon with no chores to do when one of the winners in the game let out a whoop.

"Dumb looney!" I hissed. "Mama's gonna find us, and you can just bet what's gonna happen. . ."

I never even finished my sentence. The door of the cotton house opened at that moment, and there stood Mama with a sweet gum broom in her hand, sure evidence that she had been looking for somebody to sweep the yard. Her face flushed with anger, first for being in the cotton house at all and next for what we were doing there. At sight of the cards, all her anger from days past burst out with an explosion.

"Every one of you, get yourselves out there in the yard, and you stand there until I say you can go!"

Slowly, as if doomsday had arrived, we all climbed out of the shed, wide-eyed and covered with flecks of cotton. We knew the heft of Mama's hand. This time she was unhurried, and I knew we were all in for it.

"Whose cards are these?" she asked.

No one spoke.

Mama looked slowly up and down the line of children. "An honest confession is good for the soul," she reminded.

There was still no response.

Mama took a firmer grip on the black gum brush broom, The fire of battle was in her eyes, and she intended to win. "If I don't get an answer, you're all going to take a licking. Make up your minds to it. "I've taken just about all I can, and this is the last straw." "It's cotton, Mama, not straw," I said, trying to think of the right thing to get her mind off the cards. "We were playing really carefully in it. Didn't hurt it one bit?"

149

Mama gave me a special scowl and repeated her demand. "Who owns these cards? I will not ask again."

Seeing that there was no other way to appease Mama's wrath, we waited for Charlie to speak up, but he said nothing, and we could not tattle on him. My younger sister started to cry. I thought I should shed a few tears also, but before I had time, Mama grabbed me by one arm and laid to with the broom. It was agony. I screamed as loud as I could. Four whacks, and the dozens of willowy green limbs had raised red welts all over my legs and buttocks.

"You're worse then hell and damnation both!" I screamed at Mama between sobs.

That mistake cost me two more whacks, and she went from me right on down the line. It was practically a new broom, and she all but wore it out on our backsides. She hit Charlie so hard she broke some of the twigs. I think she knew right along that the deck belonged to him. All the while, the face cards leered up at us from where the players had dropped their hands.

Mama finally decided the punishment was sufficient. She made Charlie gather up the cards. Exhausted and weeping, he did as he was told. Mama took him by the ear and led him to the cookstove. She lifted the lid and made him drop the cards into the fire. The celluloid blazed quickly in a high flame.

"Those are the devil's own game, said Mama decisively, as though her pronouncement was all it took to settle the question for all time. People go hungry because of a stack of cards like that. Men get shot. Now, All of you, get out there and do something honest with your time. Get that yard cleaned while it's damp with rain and there's no dust. If I find anything like that deck of cards again the licking you got today is just a taste. Not one of my children is going to burn in hellfire if I can help it."

I was still smarting from that licking, and my feelings poured out before I thought. "Hell can't be much worse hurting than what we just been through Charlie, so if you want to play cards, just take your pick."

Homer gabbed my arm and yanked me out of reach before Mama could recover from her shock at this outrage. "She'll beat you again if you ain't careful," Homer warned. "And that broom ain't nothing to fool with."

I knew my brother was right, but it was still hard for me to control my feelings. We stayed as far from the house as we could until Mama and I both had calmed down. Distance was the best solution when we were uncertain about the right or wrong of things.

For days afterward Mama was especially watchful of what went on around our house. It almost seemed that she took part of the blame on herself for letting the cards slip past. Maybe she felt that things had got onto a downhill path while she was away in Georgia, and it was up to her to see that they got straightened around. She would have to keep her family closer together in the future, so she could look after the physical and spiritual welfare of all of us. Clearly, in her mind, we were not up to looking after ourselves.

CHAPTER XIII

A New Job for Papa

I think we were all glad to make it through that week when Mama discovered the playing cards. By Saturday afternoon, our hurts had healed more or less and our free time was very welcome. When Homer and I heard that we might go play, we were off for a favorite spot, relieved to get away from Mama's supervision for a while.

Blue and the younger Tatums met us near our house on a steep hillside covered with white oak and pine. Here we neighborhood children had built a swing out of a discarded hoop from a wagon-wheel hub and a broken cable from Papa's saw mill. One end of the cable was fastened high in an oak tree to a stout limb. Dangling from the wheel hub at the other end, we could take a running start down the hill, swing out over the ravine at the bottom and drop into a pile of soft sand on the far side.

The Tatums greeted Homer and me with the news that they had hauled a fresh load of sand up from the creek, and we admired it from beneath the oak tree. The Tatums always had time to do such things. "Shiftless," was Mama's word for them. They never seemed to have chores to do at home the way we did.

When My turn to swing came, I soared out over the ravine like a bird in flight, sailing over the sand under a power which seemed magical, and I dared to turn loose sooner than the others. Landing lightly. The exhilarated happy feeling from a Saturday afternoon playing on the swing stayed with me clear through services on Sunday morning.

Sunday at our house meant a special flurry of activity over braids, bows and last minute chores which had somehow missed being done the day before. In spite of the bustle, or because of it, we arrived at the church with time to spare.

As usual, our preacher finished the interesting part of the morning lesson when he read the scripture. After that he rambled over some long sad tales about people dying just after or just before they had been saved. He was more impressed by the sermon than anyone else. He wept and blew his nose.

At the close of the session, he announced activities for the coming week and told news of the parish. Mrs. Watkins had had her baby, and the Allbright children were sick with measles. He asked us to remember them in our prayers, and all others in need. When he finished, he asked if anyone in the congregation had anything to add.

I stood up. He looked at me dubiously over his spectacles but nodded that I might say my piece. "Our old yeller cat had seven kittens," I said.

There was a flutter of embarrassed laughter, and people started to rise from their seats ready to leave. I knew I had better get out of there quick from the look Mama gave me. "I'll tend to you when we get home," she said, as I darted between her and our friend Aunt Matt Tudor.

"Oh, let the child be, Emma," soothed Aunt Matt. "I found what she said a relief after that sermon. If I'd had a bucket of water, I would have thrown it on him. Maybe it wouldn't have been so dry."

Sensing an ally, I took Aunt Matt's hand. "Can Homer and me eat dinner at your house?" I asked.

Aunt Matt evidently knew something about what was in store for me at home, for she turned to Mama and said, "That sounds like a real good idea Emma. Mark is away, and they can help me feed the stock."

"All right," said Mama with a look of bitter contempt. "We'll pick them up after the sing tonight."

I followed Aunt Matt happily out of the church. I had at least put off the moment of reckoning, and there was always a chance that something would happen during the afternoon to take Mama's mind off the licking she intended to give me.

Aunt Matt was not really our aunt, but we loved to go to her house. She was an old lady who had lived through the Civil War, and the stories she told us about those times were very sad but fascinating. Homer and I looked forward to hearing one after Sunday dinner.

When we arrived at Aunt Matt's, we had a surprise. Blue was waiting on her front steps wearing a pair of pants cut down from an old pair of Uncle Mark's, a sure sign it was Sunday. On other days he wore a tow shirt or ragged overalls. He was always welcome at Aunt Matt's for he carried her wood and water and helped around the farm in numerous ways. We all went into her kitchen together.

Aunt Matt knew my weaknesses in food. She had sausage, hot biscuits and molasses. She also had an omelette made with peach brandy and a pinch of some herb that gave it just the right tangy flavor.

After dinner Blue, Homer and I laid quilts on the shady end of her back porch and flopped down on our stomachs. She sat leaning back against the wall. She had to have help to get up and down.

"Tell us about the worstest time you ever had in the war, Aunt Matt," I urged.

"Child, they were all worst," Aunt Matt shook her head at the memory. "But perhaps the very worst I can remember was when we had run out of anything to eat. The soldiers had passed on after staying overnight, and they took everything eatable. All we had left was some black-eyed peas Maw had hid in a jar and buried in the smokehouse. The problem was whether to divide the peas equally or put them all in a pot and try to make a soup. There were seven of us, you see, Maw an the six of us children. I was sixteen, and the baby was six months. My brother John was the oldest man. He was ten years of age."

156

She lowered her head, and we gathered close so as not to miss a word. She continued in a far-away voice. "Maw thought we ought to pray about it, and that's what we did. We were kneeling in the kitchen thanking God for the supply of food we had, which was nothing really, or so we thought, when we heard a cow lowing, plaintive and not too far off. God was more or less forgotten in our eagerness and scramble to get outside. There by the door was a cow. She was lean and hungry, and her leg was broke, but she was an answer to a heart-rendered prayer. Where she came from or who she belonged to did not matter. We patted her and watered her, and then came the big decision: should we eat her or should we save her for milk? Maw tried to milk her, for her bag seemed to be full, but she didn't give much milk. What she did give was heated right away and given to the baby. It drank it like the starved little thing it was."

"What'd you do then, Aunt Matt?" I asked. "How'ed you all get by?" I knew the answer, of course. Homer, Blue and I had heard the story many times, but we wanted to hear it again, all the way through to the end, and Aunt Matt had a habit of dozing off if we didn't remind her that we were still listening.

"Well, child," she said. "The neighbors came over to help us. One of them happened to have some chloroform for birthing babies, and that decided us to cut off that cow's broken leg and try to save her. She couldn't have lived with it the way it was, all swollen and terrible to look at. We tied the cow down and gave her the chloroform, and Maw sawed off the leg and sewed up the stump. Then we pried the cow up on a standing framework which was padded and ready. I swear she knew just what we were doing. She didn't even moo or grunt, just calmly chewed her cud. We named her Blessed. I remember so well how it shortened to Ol' Bess." Aunt Matt sat quietly for a moment, lost in her memories.

"What's you all do with that leg?" prompted Blue.

"What do you think, child? We wuz desperate. We had that leg, and it was meat. Maw cleaned it careful and put it in the pot, added the little salt we had and started it cooking. Maw remembered where some wild onion grew in the garden of an old house and sent me to fetch a bunch back. When I got over there, a young Negro and his grandfather were living in the house. I told them what Ma had done, and the old man said, "Fetch the possum, son. We goin' over." They went back with me, and that possum was added to the cow's leg, more water, the onions and the black-eyed peas. One of the neighbors "remembered" she had a few collards. Another one had turnips and greens. Ah, you children can't know the heavenly smell of that stew. God must have heard our prayers. We all sat down to the table, and no one took more than his share. It was the best food I ever did taste."

Aunt Matt gazed off over our heads into the distance. "Ol' Bess lived a long time, she did. She really was intelligent. She learned to rest herself braced on a framework of poles. Each day we brought all the water she could drink. The old man made her a wooden leg from a gum hollow. It was crude, but light and strong. Most important, it was made with loving kindness. I don't think she held it against us that we ate her leg. I think she understood how hard we was having it."

Aunt Matt fell silent, and her head began to nod. We three looked at each other and quietly left the porch for the cover of the huge fig tree in the back yard. There, we really bawled. The story brought the sadness and hardship of those times home to us. It always did. We wiped our eyes with grimy fists and finally went to find some of Aunt Matt's chores that looked like they needed doing.

On our way to the barn, several cows watched us curiously over the pasture fence. "You sure are lucky you wasn't born back in that ol' war," said Homer. "Bet you wouldn't have come out of it with no broke leg, either, like Ol' Bess. Them soldiers would have had you all et up."

In the barn we found a sack of corn and ground some to feed Aunt Matt's chickens. We also brought in wood for her stove and fireplace. Work was more agreeable at Aunt Matt's house than at home. First, it was in return for something nice she had done for us, and second, there was nobody to tell us we had better get a move on or get a licking.

When it came evening and time for the sing, Blue said he had better be getting home. Homer and I said good-bye to him and went back to our church with Aunt Matt. Many people were already there when we arrived. The service was to feature a competition in quartet singing which brought people together from a number of different churches.

Miss Hattie Milbank came to meet us as we walked through the gate onto the church grounds. She was Mama's age and sang soprano in one of our church's quartets. I could not imagine what she wanted with Homer and me, but I soon found out. "Your papa coming tonight?" asked Miss Hattie with one of her sweetest smiles.

"Yes, ma'am," said Homer. "Far's I know."

"Oh, that's just fine," beamed Miss Hattie. "Mr. Racker is took sick, and I don't know of a soul but your papa who could fill in. Here he comes now with your mama. I'll just go over and ask him."

As she hurried away to put her plan into effect, Homer and I looked at each other and smiled. Papa sang bass beautifully, much better than Mr. Rucker in our opinion. If he sang in the competition, we might find enough about it to interest us and sit still for the whole time.

Before the contest got underway, people stood in groups around the church ground visiting while the quartets rehearsed one last time. Homer and I went from one to another getting a preview of the singing. We thought the quartet Papa was in did the best, even though he had not been able to practice with the other three members. Some of the groups seemed to do worse and worse the longer they rehearsed. Finally, the church bell rang, summoning us all inside.

There was group singing first. Then, the quartets got up one by one to perform for the congregation. Papa's was next to last. When all had had their turn, there was a pause while the judges. Conferred. It did not take them long to reach a decision. Deacon Sims came forward to announce it.

Folks, maybe this is going to sound strange, it being our church and all, but you all remember now, this ain't only what I think. Deacon Bradly from Highbridge Church was one of our judges and Miss Pratt from Seaton Methodist, and they agree with me. The best singing we heard tonight was from right here in our own congregation, Miss Hattie Milband and her group. Now, I don't mean that to say that everybody we heard wasn't good. They was. I know they've lifted up a lot of your hearts to the Lord, and that's what we're here for. I want to thank every one of them for their music and for the hard work they done preparing it, and I want to thank Miss Hattie especially. Now, let's all rise and sing 'God Be With You' for our closing hymn."

Homer and I grinned all over as we stood up to sing, and I nudged him in the ribs. We had known all along that Papa's group was going to win.

There was more visiting after the sing, and people began to drift off for home. As we were heading for our wagon with Papa in the rear, Miss Hattie kissed him soundly. "There that'll hold you till later. And thank you. We never would have won tonight if it hadn't been for you."

Mama moved in at that point, her green eyes and red hair flashing. "Mr. Crenshaw, If you don't mind, you will please help me get your children in the wagon, all seven of those present. Excuse me, Miss Hattie, but we got to be going. You know, it's too bad you didn't marry while you were young. You could have had a fine bunch of children like mine and Mr. Crenshaw's. Good evening, Miss Hattie. Mama climbed up onto the wagon seat with great dignity. Papa came around to the opposite side and got up. He was mad. He flipped the horses with the reins, and the team started so abruptly it jerked Mama back onto the seat. Papa said nothing. When the horses settled into a fast pull, Mama asked in her most appealing voice, "Did you like that kiss and hug she gave you, William?"

"Of course I did." Papa was still mad. "I'm a man, ain't I? And Hattie is a mighty winsome lady."

"That's why I don't want you going to Florida by yourself. I and the children are going with you."

"We'll discuss it at home, Emma," said Papa. "For now, you just sit quiet. You've tried my patience enough already for one evening."

Mama pulled her dust scarf over her face and said no more. Homer and I stared at each other wide-eyed. We were hardly home and unpacked from the trip to Georgia. Were we going away again? All of us? To Florida? We had to find out. If Papa and Mama were going to talk about those things after we were asleep, we would just have to stay awake, sneak down and listen to the discussion from the foot of the stairs.

When we reached the house, Homer and I were quick to spread the news among our brothers and sisters who had not attended the sing. We were met with disbelief on all sides. "You probably heard it all wrong," said Charlie.

Anna came to our rescue. "Then I guess I heard it wrong, too, Mr. Smart. I heard it the same as they did. Flo-ri-da. And if we go, there's some ol' Mary Ann that's going to find herself another beau. Mr. Charlie Crenshaw is going to be the tail end coming along behind."

That thought put Charlie in a different frame of mind. He would have liked to disbelieve Anna, but he did not quite dare. He became as anxious to learn what was happening as anyone, but when the house got quiet and we were all supposedly asleep, he was not willing to risk a licking for eavesdropping. Homer and I were the only ones who went downstairs.

Mama and Papa were in the kitchen keeping their voices low, but we could distinguish the words if we listened closely, and we did. Mama was explaining how she felt and why she felt that way. We tried to catch every word.

"Now, William, I don't deny there are possibilities being a drainage engineer on this project at Lakeland, but that's a long ways away, and I don't like it. It's not a fitting place for children from what you say."

"I said nothing about taking children, Emma." Papa's tone was firm. "I said nothing at all. You're right. A construction project ain't much place for children. That's why I plan to go alone. I got Warren, Lew Warren, to take over the sawmill, and he's a good man. The boys can run the farm, and with your help there shouldn't ..."

"Stop right there, Mr. Crenshaw! If you go, I'm going, and if I go, the children are going, so you can stop right there and make different plans all the way down the line. Sell this farm and we all go, or don't sell and we all stay here. How many women are going on this job? I'll just guess every man who goes will have his wife to protect him from - - well - - from..."

Mama did not quite knew what she was thinking. She had Hattie Milbank in mind. Mama was a jealous woman, and she was not about to let Papa out of her sight, not for a long period of time, that was sure. Homer and I stared down at our feet.

In the kitchen, Papa was understandably angry. His voice rose. "Just like a woman! Don't matter how long you live with her. Don't matter how well you treat her. She's always looking for you to be tomcatting around. I suppose you think I do that when I go to town."

"Town's got nothing to do with this," said Mama flatly. "I am talking about Florida. Whither thou goest, I will go. That's in the Bible, and that's what I'm going to do. You can make plans to that effect!"

A chair scraped on the floor as Papa stood up. "You and your quotes from the Bible! I've listened to it long enough. I'm going out. I'll be back directly."

Papas' footsteps echoed on the kitchen floor. The back door slammed. Homer and I moved too. We had learned everything we could for the time being, and Mama might come upstairs anytime to check on us. When we reached the top of the stairs, I whispered a question.

"What's a drainage engineer?"

Homer thought a moment. "Well, they go where it's swampy and get ditches dug and levees built, and that makes the swamp dry up. They use dynamite. Don't be scared of going. I bet it'll be lots of fun. Maybe better than Grandpa's."

"You really think we're going?"

"Sure we are. Don't Mama always get her way?"

That answer took care of any other questions I might have had. I knew my brother was right. If there was one person in our house who got her way, it was Mama.

Chapter XIV

To Florida by Model T

As Homer foresaw, Mama got her way about going to Florida. Papa was not about to give up a good job on the drainage project, and when he saw that Mama was equally determined to accompany him, he agreed that we should all go. He would go first to find us a house - - or have one built if there was nothing suitable. We would follow several weeks later.

With the main issue decided, Mama set off in pursuit of another objective with the same single-minded determination. "You know, William." she began one evening when we were all at the supper table. "When you think of how much money it will cost to send all of us on the train, you might as well buy a car and have something to show for the money."

Papa put down his fork rather suddenly. "What's that you say, Emma?" he asked.

Mama went through her reasoning again.

"Humph," responded Papa. "I'm surprised at you Emma. Why, I can't count the times I've heard you say the automobile was an instrument of the devil."

"I never said that, William."

"You did woman. I've heard you."

"Well, I never meant it. The Lord put us on earth to have dominion over everything here and progress, and the automobile is a sign we're doing just that. You might as well buy one for this trip to Florida, save money in the end."

"I'll study on it, Emma," said Papa.

He sounded irritated, but we children knew Mama had the battle practically won. If Papa had been really opposed to the idea of an automobile, he would have said "No!" in a voice loud enough to make waves on the gravy dish.

Mama had never actually ridden in a car, no more than any of the rest of us, so her ideas about motoring did not come from personal experience. She had indeed believed at one time that the automobile was an instrument of the devil along with playing cards and dances, but the pages of the "Woman's Home Companion" had changed her mind. The magazine showed ladies riding in motor cars wearing fashionable broad-brimmed hats and long dust veils that streamed in the wind. I had seem Mama turn those pages very slowly when she thought no one was watching her. I knew from the wistful expression on her face that she would like to be one of those ladies. The move to Florida was her chance to make that dream come true.

Mama mentioned the car frequently in the days that followed. Papa replied to her hints with a grunt or a mutter, but she was not discouraged. She suggested that the older girls might like to make themselves dust coats so they could ride in style if their father decided to buy the automobile. They did not need much urging to set to work, and their hemming and measuring went forward enthusiastically, especially when Papa was around. He pretended not to notice.

Then, one morning Papa got up from the breakfast table and said casually to the two oldest boys, "Cal, Charlie? You have that team ready?"

"Yes, Pa," answered Charlie.

"Well, best get moving then. Get them horses to ol' man Hayes, and bring back that infernal machine your mother sets so much store by. Got to get to Florida sometime."

"William!" Mama beamed at him across the table. "I was just sure you'd do it."

"You gonna sell the horses, Papa?" asked Homer.

"Not exactly, son. Gonna trade 'em on that Model T Ford. We can't take 'em to Florida with us, that's for sure. Mr. Hayes is a good Christian man. He won't sell 'em to nobody mean."

Papa went out with the older boys. Homer and I looked at each other with long faces. We were excited about the car as anyone, but Blue Boy and Cotton Top had been part of our family for as long as we could remember. We had always shelled corn for them and put down hay. It made us sad to think the automobile would take their place completely.

Mama did not give us long to brood. She sent Homer and me out to sweep the yard while the older girls finished their dust caps. When chores were done, she declared a sort of holiday. We all had to bathe, wear clean clothes and sit around waiting for Papa and the boys to return.

Homer and I sat on the barnyard fence to listen for the sound of the new automobile. Soon, we heard a putt-putt far down the road. "Hear that?" shouted Homer, excited. "Boy, we ever gonna show that ol' Maybelle something. We got the first car of anybody anywheres around here."

The main road and the shady, gully-washed lane which led back to our house were not designed for cars. When the Model T came in sight with Papa driving, it appeared lop-sided from the way it sat in the ruts. Cal and Charlie waved as they approached and watched to see how the family was reacting.

Papa was not yet too well versed in handling the car. He missed the turn into the yard. "Whoo!" he yelled, but the car kept straight on and was only stopped by running into the fence around the pig lot at the far end of the lane. The experience shook the menfolk a little, but they soon recovered. Papa took a look at the damage and said he could fix things at the mill blacksmith shop in no time at all.

While the car was undergoing its repairs, getting a fender straightened mostly, we all gathered round to admire it. It was a beauty, black shiny metal with new smelling leather seats. It had side curtains, two carriage lamps and two headlights. The wheels had red spokes. Mama was so thrilled by it she did not even scold

Homer and me when we got finger marks on the fender. She just took Charlie's bandana and rubbed the smudged place until it shone again.

As soon as the car was fixed, Papa drove Mama and the older girls on their first ride. They were all dressed in their new riding outfits, and I had never seen Mama sit so straight and tall. As they drove off, she practiced waving at those of us who were left behind. She barely nodded and lifted her hand in a haughty way. When they were safely out of sight, I imitated her, and we all fairly busted, laughing. Maybe it was for the best that we were moving to Florida. If Mama was going to wave at other people like that, we would soon get the name of being snobs here in Arkansas.

Homer and I did not get our first ride in the car until much later in the afternoon. Charlie drove, and we sat in the back seat with Anna between us. The car bumped and jolted over the ruts as we started out the lane, and being in the middle Anna had nothing much to hold on to. Before we got to the main road, she was crying with fright and begging to get out.

"All right!" yelled Charlie. He was mad. He had to stop the car, and stopping and starting were not his best maneuvers. He managed, however.

Anna scrambled out and ran back toward the house crying, "Charlie's trying to kill me!"

Homer and I had the brace rod for the top to hold onto, so we were not troubled as much by the jolting. When Charlie got out on the main road, we were exhilarated by the wind on our faces as we whizzed through the countryside at twelve to fifteen miles an hour.

Mama had told us to sit with our hands in our laps as we traveled along, but that was almost an impossibility. If You were planning to go far, you had to hold on for dear life. With roads the way they were, it was a miracle if you could sit for more than a minute without assistance from somewhere.

When we came to the Hoglin farm, the whole family rushed out to see who was passing, for a car was a novelty. Charlie made the thing chug-a-lug right up to their gate. When they all jumped back, he stopped so they could admire the car.

I preened and acted as nearly like Mama as I could, nodding at Maybelle without a word. Homer jumped out and thrust his hands into his high-pocket pants. "It's just a car," he said with a lordly tone. "Most people can afford one these days." I was sure he was repeating something the salesman had said to Charlie or Papa in town.

Maybelle moved over as close to Homer as she could and said cuttingly, "You can't steer it, can you little boy?" Then she came up to the side of the car by Charlie and sweetly asked, "Oh, Mr. Crenshaw! Please, may I please have a ride in your beautiful automobile?"

"Course," said Charlie promptly. "Anna was afraid, so you can sit in back by Homer and Ressie."

Disappointed, for she had hoped to sit in front with him, Maybelle climbed over me and sat down. We started with a jerk that tossed her back against the cushion. She grabbed first one of us, then the other. Finally, seizing the right moment, she sat forward and held onto Charlie, fairly choking him. "You sure know a lot about automobiles," she cooed. "And it takes a strong man to handle one of these fast things."

Charlie glowed.

Homer and I were glad to get Maybelle delivered back home. The next visit was more welcome to us. We asked Charlie to give Blue a ride in the car, And he was agreeable. We drove down to Pair-O-Dice.

Blue and his family were impressed with the automobile, but he and Granny Paradise were the only ones who decided they wanted a ride. The others might have been scared off by Charlie telling them we only had the car for one day. Hearing that could have shaken their confidence in his driving.

Granny might not have had any confidence in Charlie either, but she had faith in her spells. When she got settled among her skirts in the front seat, she took out a bag of charms. Holding onto one of them, she said loud enough for us to hear, "These wheels like the win' will carry ma kin, and some day I swear, they'll fly through the air. On wheel and on wing, a flying machine," she nodded emphatically. "That so! Bible, it say that. Preacher, he done read them words. I's ready in a minute soon as I sprinkle this safe powder round 'bout. You ain't gonna get hurt in this con-trap-shun, boy. It's a safe charm."

She hung a tooth of some animal and a few tail hairs tied with red string to the windshield brace, and we were ready to start. As we bumped and jolted along the road, Blue sat back holding to Homer's arm on one side and mine on the other. All he could say was, "Golly dam gee! This is for me. When I get big, gonna buy me a rig."

After the ride with Granny and Blue, Charlie drove us home. I thought the tail hair charm would go as soon as Mama caught sight of it, but she did not disturb it in any way. It hung from the windshield brace the whole time the menfolk were learning to drive the car. Between that charm and the Ford manual, Papa, Cal and Charlie more or less mastered the art of driving without serious mishap.

Purchase of the Model T was the sign that preparations for our move to Florida were shifting into high gear. We sold everything but the household goods. People came by almost daily to bid us good-bye and see what they might have for the asking, "since you can't take it with you." There was little left after we had rented a boxcar and packed it with tools and household furniture.

Papa left for Florida by train before all was ready for our departure. Mama supervised the final details amid squabbling, shoving and yelling. Those things we wished to keep but could not take with us were stored in a house Papa owned on a small acreage. One of Papa's sisters would look after it for us while we were gone. Chickens were cooped to be sold to Mr. Payne, the peddler. Special care went into finding new homes for favorite animals, Boo the boar pig, and Pumper the sow, with her nine little ones.

Homer and I had some animals and fowls that were our own. We had no problem disposing of them. We gave them to Blue and helped him build coops for them. My seven ducks could not have found a better home. Pair-O-Dice was on the bank of a creek, and we helped Blue build a pond for them.

When the animals were settled in their new home, the three of us walked slowly along the road toward our house. Never, we felt, would we find a friend like Blue in Florida, but Homer and I were not quite sure how to tell him that. Our hearts were heavy. His was too, apparently. He finally found something to say, but it was not very cheerful.

I knowed something bad was gonna buck up to me when I done killed that ol' blacksnake. He ain't never done no harm to me, but I just plain up and chop his head clean off 'fore I thought. Now, you all's going to Florida. See there? That's what happens when you don't pay no mind to spells and charms and jinxes. They just goes right to work."

"What's you kill that snake for?" asked Homer, not faulting Blue exactly, just wanting to know the cause of our misfortune. "You sure fixed it for us. We gotta move, and Lord knows if we gonna find someone else who can get us out of everything and keep trouble from happening to us like you can."

I nodded. I was really scared because Blue was someone we relied on. No matter what problem we had, he always knew something that might work to get us out of it. He looked from one of us to the other and gulped.

"Well I reckon I done thought of that, and so I brung you these here." Blue handed Homer and me each a round, shiny horse chestnut on which was carved the image of a face. "You just keep it in your pocket, and there ain't nothing real bad gonna happen to you. But then if'n it do, I only got one of these. It's the bone of a live turtle. Pa cut his leg off and give me one. So's I'm gonna give it to you. It'll take care of anything."

Blue held out the bone. He dropped his head as if parting with it was a sad thing for him. Homer was reluctant to take it.

"Me and Ressie will be all right without it," he said. "Since it's your onliest one."

"Naw, here." Blue pressed the bone into Homer's hand. "If I really need one, I'll steal Granny's for a while. 'Till I get straightened out."

"Thanks, Blue,"we said in chorus. Both Homer and I were concerned because we knew how much store he set by his charms. At the same time we were also relieved, for now we knew everything would go well with us.

"Now, 'fore I forget," Blue continued. "I wants to pass on a few helpful things." He paused to cross himself and bow three times, so the sprits or whatever, would not hold what he was telling us against him. "Now, remember. If you all gets in deep trouble, you just find a jackass and pull three hairs outed his tail. Tie the ends with one of your own hairs, and when whoever's causing you the trouble ain't looking, you just touch his left shoulder and you got him. If'n that jackass die though, you best look out!"

Blue hardly paused for breath, "And if you start somewhere and ol' jackrabbit cross your path., you just better turn your hat around once on your head. Or else make a cross where you done turned and put a stone in the center. Won't no bad luck come your way then. And if'n you wants to stay well, put a nutmeg on a string around your neck. You may have to let that work whilst you sleep. And don't you all never step on no piece of bread 'cause that is a sure sign of hellfire coming your way. Or worse yet, going hungry."

Homer and I listened open-mouthed in wonderment as Blue divulged these mysteries. Our knees trembled at the thought that we might forget something. Blue never seemed to have bad luck, and if he did, he always could explain it away and make it seem reasonable.

"'Member, too." Blue became even more serious, if that was possible. "If the cow moos after midnight, look out. Bad luck for sure. Someone gonna die! And when that ol' owl say, 'Whoo? Whoo? Whoo are you?' you say your name real fast, or he gonna pick somebody else to make wise. You'll see, If'n you don't know what to do about something, you just listen for ol' owl to ask, 'Whoo?' and you say real quick 'Homer' or 'Ressie.' Right then you think out loud what's bothering you, and ol' owl gonna say in your mind what to do. Now, I done told you all I dast. Just one more thing. When you all hear that ol' meadowlark singing his heart out, that gonna be from me to you. You all gonna say, 'Hi, Blue. Misses you.' And ol' meadowlark, he gonna fly right back here to that ol' cow pasture, and he gonna tell me what you all said. That's a fact."

Tears shimmered in Blue's eyes by now. Without waiting for our promise that we would think of him every time we saw the meadowlark, he turned and ran. The last we saw of him was the ragged behind of a pair of blue overalls going over a rail fence.

That was our good-bye visit with Blue. The last few days before our departure for Florida were filled with packing and visiting from morning to night. It was decided that Homer and I would ride in the car with Mama and Anna. Charlie would drive. The rest of the family, including the twins, would go by train under the guardianship of Cal, whom Mama considered the most reasonable and steady of the older boys.

It would have been nice to see Blue wave good-bye to us as we pulled out of the yard, but he was not there, and we knew better than to really wish for it. It was dreadful bad luck for someone to make a special effort to see you off on a long trip. It meant you would never see them again.

At the station, we said good-bye to those of the family who were going by train. Mama was nervous about the separation, but there was no help for it. She could not travel with both sets of us, and for better or worse she had chosen the car. She gave the older girls many parting instructions about the care of the twins. Finally, the train got up steam and pulled out. Our adventure with the automobile began.

In the beginning Mama did not know one thing about cars. She simply liked to be seen riding in one, fashionably dressed, and she did not want any problems while so doing. Before the first week of the trip was over, she learned that the "Woman's Home Companion" had neglected to mention certain things about motoring, notable among them being restless children, infrequent places to buy gasoline and bad roads.

Where the roads were good, Charlie could make from twelve to fifteen miles an hour, but most places they were terrible. Homer and I often ran along beside or behind the car, and we had no trouble keeping up. There were mud holes and sand bars for the car to get stuck in, and after a rain the dirt roads were always gully-washed. Several times the car almost tipped over. Mama would glare at Charlie whenever that happened, but she did not utter one word of complaint.

By contrast, Anna whimpered constantly, even when Homer and I were running along behind the car and she had the back seat to herself. Mama finally got tired of it. She yanked Anna out of the car at a rest stop and gave her hallelujah hell. Homer and I clapped our hands over our mouths to keep from laughing out loud. Anna was one of Mama's favorites. She very seldom got the kind of treatment we were accustomed to.

"This was your choice to come along," shrilled Mama. "You could have ridden the train, and I wish the Lord you had, but no! You had to ride in the car with me. Well, you're here, and you can hush that whining right now. If you don't there's willow brush in every creek bottom we come to. Charlie can just stop the car and cut me a switch. Do you hear me? Now, you sit there in that seat and shut your mouth."

Anna whimpered a little in response, but she was quieter after that.

Of an evening, we would stop pretty much wherever we were and pitch a lean-to tent against the car. We gathered wood for a fire to boil coffee and fry bacon and eggs when necessary, but many evenings we were invited for supper at a neighboring house. People wanted to hear all about what it was like to travel by car. They were glad to trade a meal, sometimes a night's lodging also for the chance to satisfy their curiosity. Mama was in her element on these occasions. She basked in the attention of her audience and made like motoring was nothing really.

We camped one night on the edge of a village. While we were sitting around the fire, three men came and plundered through our belongings. Mama had money for the trip hidden somewhere in the car, but they did not find it. They were looking for a man they said, and ran away.

I was too scared to sleep well after that. I dozed for a while, then awakened. Charlie was sitting by the fire. A man was with him. They spoke in low tones.

"Please, mister," said the stranger. "I'm hungry. I ain't et nothing for three days."

I saw Charlie give him coffee and what food was cooked. He nodded gratefully.

"Thanks, mister. I wuz just going through that town, and they jailed me. There wuz talk of putting me on the chain gang, and when I saw my chance, I got away. I ain't done nothing but knock out the old guy that brought me food. I sure wuz hungry, too, but I ran. Been hiding in the woods. Gonna go back to my folks in Louisiana. Sure wish I'd stayed there."

"Good luck," said Charlie. "Maybe you best go on when you can though. I got some of my little brothers and sisters with me. Can't afford to have no trouble."

As soon as the man finished eating, he slipped quietly into the woods. Thinking of Cousin Feaster and the chain gang I had seen at Grandpa's, I prayed they wouldn't catch him.

The weather was unsettled for most of the trip, sometimes rain, sometimes hot sun. It started to rain one evening about dark. Mama decided we should eat cold food and keep going until we reached a town, but we had to put up the side curtains first. Their storage place was under the seats. By the time they were up, everyone was soaked to the skin.

From past experience we knew the roads were not well marked. We had often gone miles on the wrong road before discovering our mistake. Now, in the rain, we did not dare pass a single marker, and it was hard to see them along the road ahead. At each sign, one person had to get out to read what the sign said. Homer usually did this. He was good at it. In pouring rain he ran to read a sign partly hidden by brush. Suddenly, a train shooshed by. Mama was sure Homer had been run over and began calling his name. I was afraid that he would not answer.

"I'm alright," came Homer's voice from the rain. A moment later he stood before us, covered with mud, a sorry sight. The only bright spots picked up by the carbide lamps of the car were two merry eyes.

"That there sign says, 'Railroad crossing, watch out for the cars.' I seen the train coming just in time and I jumped. There's a ravine beside the track."

He climbed in the back seat again. I wiped his face and held him close. I knew how scared he must have been. The others laughed with relief.

Altogether the trip to Florida required four weeks. The first week was real fun for us. The second was interesting, the third uninteresting, and the fourth pure hell. I was boney. My arms and buttocks grew raw from constant rubbing on leather. Sulfur water and goat butter upset my stomach. My head ached, and all I could think of was a soft pillow and my own bed. Homer held me and let me rest my head on his shoulder. I slept from time to time in spite of the jolting of the car.

Since Charlie was just becoming familiar with automobiles and their care, we bought three tires and inner tubes before we reached our destination. Once the car stalled completely, much to Mama's disgust. "What's the matter now?" she asked Charlie in irritation.

"It's hot Ma," he replied. "It'll go again in a bit. We got water for it, and there's a breeze now and then."

Mama was not about to sit in the hot sun waiting on the car's convenience. We were in a sandy part of the road, and the shade was a mile or more away. Another car passing us was very unlikely, so Mama did the only thing she could. Scolding and jerking, she marched us along to the shade.

It felt like it was over a hundred degrees. The sand was deep and difficult to walk in, especially with us carrying all the stuff Mama felt she must have along. Homer and I took some comfort from the fact that it was easier on us than on Anna. We ran all day in the sun and sand at home, though not dressed in our best clothes. Sand sifted into our shoes, and sweat ran in rivulets.

We were all thirsty by the time we reached the shade, and we discovered that our oasis was already occupied. Mosquitoes met us, covering us in their eager anticipation. There was nothing we could do about the mosquitoes, but Mama saw a solution to the other problem. There was a spring of water visible at a small house down the road a piece. She sent Homer and me to get a pail.

A woman stood in the doorway of the house as we approached. She stared at us as if we were apparitions. "May we have some water?" I asked as nicely as I knew how.

The woman looked us over and retreated toward the back of the small shack. "Jude, cum a-running," she almost screamed.

A tall man, sunburnt and wrinkled, wearing patch-on-patched overalls came to the door. A hound dog wagged it's tail at his appearance and flopped down in the shade of the porch. The man spat a squirt of brown juice toward the dog. "I do swear," he said. "You'uns get loosed around here or sumpin?"

"We need water," I stated.

"Well now, we got plenty," he said, indicating a bucket on the porch. "Hep yourself."

Homer and I took a drink from the gourd dipper and almost gagged at the sulfur taste. The man threw hack his head and laughed. "Just can't hep having a little fun," he said after a minute, by way of apology. "You'uns from Georgia?"

"Nope," said Homer. "Arkansas. Our automobile broke down, and my brother's fixing it now. Our mother's sitting down there a piece in the shade. She'd like a drink of water."

The man took a wooden pail from the shelf on the porch. "We got fresh water out back," he said. Barefoot, unmindful of the sand spurs and scorpions, he went somewhere out behind the shack and returned with a pail full of water. It was sweet and cold. He gave us each a drink, then picked up the pail, took a gourd dipper hanging by the door and strode off down the hot, dusty road without a word.

Mama could be charming when she wanted to be, and by the time we returned with the man, she had simmered down enough to appreciate a drink of fresh water, even if it was not so cool after being carried through the hot sun.

"You're very kind," she said. She wiped her sweaty face leaving streaks of dust. She really looked like a lost little girl, and I could see why Papa was so stuck on her. The man was impressed too.

"My pleasure, ma'am," he said. "I see there's skeeters here botherin' you. Just you let me rub some of this on. And them ol' skeeters will plain leave you alone."

He took a bottle from his hip pocket and poured some oily substance into his palm. He rubbed it on my mother's neck and offered her some for her hands and face. I think he decided he better not touch her too much.

He poured some of the liquid into our hands, too, and we rubbed it all over our faces, necks and hands. It smelled vile, but it worked.

The man stretched his long frame against the trunk of a sycamore tree and gazed hungrily at my mother. I don't know how he managed to make small talk, but he did. "Them cantankerous automobiles sure causes people a sight of trouble, I hear. Ain't never rid in one myself. My ol' mule, he may get outta whack now and then, but a dose of liniment fixes him right off."

Freed from swatting mosquitoes and refreshed by the water, Mama had spread a small blanket of the baby's on the ground and relaxed graciously, imitating a picture out of the "Woman's Home Companion." "My son is very efficient," she said. "He'll have the car ready before long. We're going to Lakeland."

"Lake-Land. Well, ain't that sumpin." The man stretched out a foot and almost touched mama's hand. "That your boy, huh? And you look 'bout twenty yourself."

That did it. Mama preened and smiled and fluffed her hair which was only slightly streaked with gray. She started in on her regular line of chatter. Evidently the man was hungry for any kind of talk. He listened and looked his fill. I think Mama never enjoyed herself so much.

Charlie finally got the car started again and drove up with a broad grin. He thanked the man for bringing the pail of water and asked if he wanted a lift back to the house.

I thought at first that he was going to refuse, but the temptation was too great; a ride in an automobile and in front with Charlie and Mama. He melted into the narrow space, grasping the side brace with one arm and extending the other along the back of the seat around Mama. I could see his hand was stiff with excitement. He spat tobacco out on the hot sand. Steam rose and died, leaving a brown spot on the ground.

Charlie stalled the car about half way to the house and had to get out to crank it. The man threw hack his head and laughed loud and louder, until we laughed with him.

"What's so funny?" asked Mama.

"I wuz just thinking, ma'am. If my ol' mule had his tail in front, I could wind him up and he'd take off, too."

It was a funny notion. We all laughed again.

We stopped at his house. His woman stood clenching hold of the door frame, wide-eyed and scared, as if she thought we might take him with us. She stepped out and back like a new dance, first on one foot, then on the other.

The car stopped with a puff and stalled again. We had to get water for it and drinking water for us.

"Is it dead, hun?" called the woman from the porch.

Charlie explained that we just needed cool water. We filled the car, all the occupants and a two gallon crock jug. Having fresh spring water in abundance, Mama washed her face. The man stood a long time looking at her.

"Ma'am, it's been a real pleasure," he said. "I done almost forgot the likes of you ever existed. You done brought me luck. Tomorrow I'm riding to town. Gonna get me a job, buy my woman a new dress. Deed I am! Then get me an automobile. Even if'n it quits sometime, it's better than my ol' mule."

As we drove away, the man and woman moved out into the road. He waved his old slouch hat, arms flaying back and forth.

"Good thing Papa went by train," said Homer in a whisper.

"Was Mama sparking him?" I whispered back.

"Yeah, you could say that. Papa and Hattie Milbank weren't nothing."

Just then, the car hit a rocky place and jolted something fierce, throwing me against the side. When I straightened up, I felt a fresh bruise coming. I hoped the trip to Florida was just about over. I did not think my scrapes and bruises could take much more.

Chapter XV

Okahumpka

It developed that Mama had not spoken very precisely when she said we were going to Lakeland. Our actual destination was the small town of Okahumpka further North. Hungry and tired from driving in the heat and mosquitoes, we arrived about two in the afternoon, and the town rolled slowly past the moving car. A building that smelled strongly of resin which Charlie said was a turpentine still, several large frame houses, the depot, the post office, several stores and a hotel. On the steps of the hotel stood Papa waiting for us, a welcome sight, indeed. Mama practically fell out of the car into his arms.

"Yes, Emma," he soothed in response to her questions. "They all got here safe and sound. I think they were a little sorry to leave their grandparents is all. The twins are fine. I've taken more rooms at the hotel for you."

"Where?" asked Mama in surprise.

"Here at the hotel. You and the children will stay there until the house is finished. You will have three rooms on the second floor."

"William, whatever are you thinking of? All these children in a hotel!"

Papa was firm, "Best thing for them, and I'll be in town on weekends."

"But what's the matter with the house?"

"The men are building a veranda surrounding it, and I'm having it screened. You simply can't stay out there until the screens are up. You've had a taste of what it's like coming through the swamps."

"He right, ma'am," confirmed a man who had been talking with Papa as we drove up and was apparently connected with the construction project in some way. "You move out there before we uns get them screens on, ol' skeeters eat you up."

Mama swatted at one of those insects which had just landed on her sleeve. "Yes," she muttered. "I've a pretty good idea they might."

Mosquitoes were bad enough on the steps of the hotel, and flies swarmed around us, too. Mama gave in to the situation, but she made it plain that she was not happy about it. As we climbed out of the car, she yanked me by the arm to relieve her feelings and slapped Homer for no other reason. "Well, let's see those rooms," she said to Papa. "I could do with a bit of hot water after that road."

Seeing that the crisis was over, Papa turned from Mama to the rest of us. He welcomed Anna and me with a hug apiece and gave

Homer and Charlie man-to-man handshakes. Charlie received a special commendation for getting the car to Okahumpka more or less in one piece.

Since there were more boxes and bags than we could handle easily, Papa pressed into service the fellow he had been talking with as we drove up, a man called Big Jack. Following Mama and the manager of the hotel, we made a procession upstairs to the rooms Papa had reserved for us. The brothers and sisters we had not seen since leaving Arkansas were all there, and everyone talked at once, bringing the others up to date on what had been happening while we were separated. The noise awakened the twins who promptly began to cry. Papa and one of the older girls went to hush them.

Homer and I were enthralled by our new quarters. We had never stayed in a hotel before. When the manager had finished showing Mama over the rooms and gone back downstairs, we went on our own tour, opening wardrobe doors, looking under beds and pulling window blind cords. Our exploration was interrupted by the arrival of two Negro bellboys carrying a bushel basket of grapefruit and oranges.

"What's this?" asked Mama, ever alert for an unnecessary expenditure of money.

"Compliments of the management, ma'am," said one of the boys.

"Take those back! We can't afford them." Mama tried to stop the boys with the command, but as if their lives depended on delivering the basket, they set it down quickly and ran. It fell to Papa to do the reassuring.

"Don't worry, Emma. It's all taken care of. The fruit grows out in back, and if they didn't give it away, they couldn't get rid of it. It's tree ripened and can't be shipped."

"Oh, well. In that case." At the prospect of getting something for free, Mama calmed down right away.

Papa had been fussing with the babies. Now, he turned to Big Jack and handed him some money. "Would you get a bag of sugar, Jack?" he asked. "And have the manager send up a knife and some spoons."

We were soon enjoying a wonderful treat, for oranges and grapefruit were delicacies we usually saw only at Christmas. Homer and I decided right then that Florida was not all bad, even if it did possess an overabundance of sulfur water and mosquitoes.

The hotel had an indoor toilet bath on the second floor, and Mama quickly laid claim to it for at least the two hours it would take to get her family in a presentable condition. The manager told her to bring us down for dinner at 5:30, and by that time we were all bathed and dressed in clean clothes. The clothes were slightly wrinkled to be sure, but when we went down the broad stairs all together, I still felt Mama and Papa could be proud of us. I know it was a proud moment for me. From the way the other guests looked at us, we were the center of attention, and for once Mama did not feel the need to reprimand any one of us for appearance or behavior.

In addition to transient guests, salesmen and the like, the hotel also served as a sort of boarding house for the men hired on the construction project and the two teachers from the local grammar school, Miss Flossie Chitwood and Miss Novella Magby. All seemed to have their regular places at the long tables in the dining room, and Papa found seats for us. He introduced a few people to Mama, but there was not time for much of that before dinner was served.

The food was plentiful. We had chicken and dumplings, crisp fried seafood, a basket of hush puppies, fresh green peas and a salad of some unfamiliar greens, chopped fine. There was also fresh fruit galore, papayas and various melons. Homer and I ate until we were stuffed.

After dinner, we offered no protest when Mama told us it was our bedtime. Tired, our appetites satiated and nothing to watch rolling past the car, we climbed into clean beds and were instantly asleep. The last thing I heard was Papa's voice. "I'm glad you're here, Emma. I've missed you. It's good to have us all here together."

The hotel visit proved to be a lark for Homer and me. Up at dawn, we were on the go until Mama insisted on our going to bed early in the evening - - where she thought we stayed. This was not so. As soon as she was safely downstairs, we were up and onto the roof of the veranda where we could see and hear what went on below us through the chinks.

Most of the guests gathered on the veranda in the evening. The big fan there turned slowly, stirring the hot air. It was a symbol only because until the sun sank behind the forest, there was never any cooling effect, it was only from the stir of air against sweating bodies.

Not long after our arrival, Mama decided she and the older girls would have to wear fewer underskirts. Three was simply too many in the sultry Florida weather. One afternoon she convened a family conference on the subject in our hotel suite. Homer and I were interested observers.

"This is being a bit bold," said Mama, "but circumstances alter cases, and this heat is more than I ever thought possible. Walk with your legs close together and don't spread them when you're sitting down. You can let the edge of the slip you're wearing show just a teeny bit. That way, people will know you are properly dressed."

Having reached this point, Mama felt a demonstration was in order. She pulled her top skirt up a wee bit and sat down to show the girls how it should be done. They blushed and looked embarrassed, and Elinor, the oldest, protested that she would feel naked going downstairs dressed like that.

Mama was firm in spite of all objections. She had several daughters to marry off and was not about to miss the opportunity offered for displaying her wares. She knew, as did Homer and I, that the girls were well on the way to finding beaus among the guests at the hotel, and since they all seemed eligible young men, Mama saw nothing to discourage about the situation. Later that evening, we watched our sisters descend the stairs, walking stiff-legged and shy in their new style of attire. We hurried to the roof of the veranda as soon as we could and found chinks for ourselves where we could see what went on.

Our sisters were frightfully self-conscious in their single underskirts, but their admirers did not seem to notice anything wrong. Two of the older girls cast nervous glances at two of the young construction workers, room numbers Eight and Ten. Elinor sat a little apart from the others with her potential beau. She was stuck on a traveling salesman who had only one arm. His line of talk made up for his shortages elsewhere. He never stopped as long as anyone would listen, which was all right for Ellie. She never said much.

As days went by, our whole family profited from Elinor's blossoming acquaintance with David. He sold notions, a fact that struck Homer and me as peculiar when we first heard it. Up to that time we had always thought of a notion in terms of "I gotta notion," but David put us straight with a look into his sample case. Mama bought a number of things from him. She was confident he would not cheat her, a trust she did not always have in the people she traded with.

Homer and I shared in the benefits from the atmosphere of general goodwill. David gave us each a free gift of our choice, "for the children of my good customers," as he put it with a wink. Homer got a Jew's harp. I chose a Kewpie doll.

Besides the guests of the hotel, some of the townspeople also came to enjoy the veranda of an evening. Mrs. Teagardener was one of those who found numerous excuses to join the group. She was a young widow, well built, with large blue eyes and an abundance of blondish hair which she wore upswept in a pug held with a tortoise shell comb. Like a nervous hummingbird, she was never still but twitched and flitted from one vacant chair on the veranda to the next.

The construction men teased each other about her, making jokes, even in her presence, but she took it all good naturedly. She made it obvious that she was looking for a new husband and most any man would do. She would sit gazing with adoring blue eyes at any man willing to talk to her, and she somehow always managed to touch him in her nervous way, a pat on the shoulder or a hand on the knee. Fascinated, my brother and I watched her from the veranda roof.

"Bet she was sparking Papa 'fore we got here," whispered Homer.

Noticing that Mrs. Teagardener had Papa off to one side of the veranda, I asked, "Ain't she doing that now?"

Homer shook his head. "Not like she could," he said with a knowledgeable air.

Mama did not miss what was going on either, and it made her simply furious, though she tried hard to be a lady about the whole thing. She kept a sharp eye on the situation on the veranda and made a point of rescuing Papa whenever she thought he needed it. Mad as she was, I think she was satisfied in a way about the turn of events. With women like Mrs. Teagardener to contend with, it was clear she had made the right decision in coming to Florida.

What with two teachers living right there in the hotel and the school being nearby, it was not long before Mama decided Homer and I should be attending class. We were apprehensive at first about the idea, remembering Miss Harris back in Arkansas, but there was no arguing with Mama, and we went to school. We were pleasantly surprised.

Miss Flossie did not punish us as much as Miss Harris had. In fact, we were among her favorite pupils. It was not so much that we excelled in our studies as that we came regularly and therefore her teaching had a chance to take effect. Most of the children came on a hit and miss basis as their parents felt like sending them or they felt like coming. Whether Homer and I felt like coming or not, Mama always felt like sending us.

The schoolhouse was small, two rooms with handmade benches and desks. The blackboard in our classroom was slate divided by a strip of wood. It was cracked anglewise on the left side. The remaining equipment consisted of two erasers, an American flag, a picture of George Washington and another called "The Potato Pickers," a calendar and a roll up map.

Miss Flossie's desk was a boughten one which sat in one corner of the room. She kept it neat and tidy. Lined up along the side of it were story books: Mrs. Wiggs of the Cabbage Patch, Aesop's Fables, Grimm's Fairy Tales and others. She read to us as part of the class work if we all had good lessons.

At first Homer and I had a lot of trouble understanding the other children, for they did not seem to speak English, at least not the way we did. Thanks to the school, however, we soon had the knack of it, much to Mama's disgust. We could distinguish all the variations of "she karn't," ranging from "she cares not to" at one end to "I won't let her" at the other. We learned that a dry land terrapin was a "cooter" because he had his house or cottage on his back. We called warts "werts" and eggplant "yeggplan." Mama tried to correct us at first, but after a while she gave up the attempt, and we talked like the other children in Okahumpka.

Between attending school and living in the hotel, Homer and I were soon acquainted with dozens of people. All of them were friendly, and none seemed too concerned about clothes which was wonderful to us. I spent most of my days wearing a short shift and a pair of flour-sack drawers. Homer wore coveralls and short-sleeved shirts. In Florida, Mama was free from the need to compete with cousins and neighbors over how her children were dressed, and she let us be free, too.

Outside of school hours, Homer and I had leisure to explore the town. There was a general store, a blacksmith shop, a post office, the depot and a small store at the edge of town that sold candy and toys. It stayed open when the general store was closed, and its penny candy and two penny toys were our biggest temptations.

At the other end of town from the candy store and situated well away from any dwellings was the turpentine still. From all appearances, it was the main reason for the town's existence. The black people worked there and many of the white people as well. Pitch was gathered from the tall pine trees and distilled into turpentine which was then shipped out in barrels to some other place for refining. I rather enjoyed the smell, from a distance, but I could understand why no one wanted to live too close to it all the time.

Attending Sunday services in Okahumpka was an interesting experience. The small clapboard church had a bell too big for the belfry, and each time it rang everyone inside the church felt as though they were being torn apart from head to foot and rocked at the same time. Many of the congregation who stayed after Sunday

194

school for church stuck their fingers in their ears until the last tone subsided.

The minister took advantage of the temporary deafness the bell created to emphasize the name of the deity. He would start to speak before people had fully recovered their hearing, and his opening sentence usually went like this. "We are gathered together here to pay tribute and praises to GOD." Hearing was fully restored only on the last word, and it burst in upon the congregation with startling force. Homer and I did not find any more of interest in the sermons than we had at home, but the effect of the bell was something we looked forward to from week to week.

During the time we stayed in Okahumpka, none of its wonders had a chance to become stale or commonplace. Always eager to see something new, Homer and I spent hours running in and out and up and down stairs at the hotel, to the extent that the manager was probably glad to see Papa come to claim us when our house was finished. At least, he helped haul our luggage downstairs with the help of one boy, a thing we had never seen him do for any other guest.

Papa came for us in a car big enough to accommodate the entire family and all our boxes. The car belonged to the company, but our pride was no less because of that, Mama's especially. She was so delighted she even spoke kindly to me. "Run, dear, and get into the automobile." She pushed me as she always did, but for once it was a gentle push.

I glowed with happiness getting into the car. It did not take anything away from my state of mind when I overheard one of the hotel guests say to another, "You know, that child is really attractive."

As Papa drove away from Okahumpka for the construction site, the last thing to catch my eye was the sign on the hotel. It was called the Laster Hotel, but the final two letters had fallen from the sign, leaving the word "Last" in faded gold capitals. It somehow struck me as being an appropriate end for our visit there.

CHAPTER XVI

New Friends – – New Problems

A little beyond the outskirts of Okahumpka, we came to the end of the hard surface road. From there on it was sand and more sand. The worst places were paved with thick poles laid across the road. They kept the car from miring into the sand but were also good for a rough ride.

Houses became fewer and further apart as we left town behind. The swamps closed in on us, thick undergrowth, palmettos and huge trees hung with Spanish moss. One tree looked like an old woman with long stringy hair and a dog beside her. Homer and I searched for other pictures in the trees ahead and reached out to touch the moss as we drove past.

A snake slithered across the road, and brilliantly-colored birds flew up out of the brush, frightened by the approach of the car. Homer and I were thrilled at each new sight and sound, but a look at Mama's face warned us not to make our enthusiasm too plain. Mama was obviously not forming a very favorable idea of our new home, and she was liable to slap anyone who disagreed with her.

Our new house was only two and a half miles from Okahumpka, but it seemed much further through the sand, the heat and the thick vegetation. It seemed like we were entering another world. Finally Papa turned off the road along the drainage canal, and there we were in our own yard. We all piled out of the car to have a look around.

The house consisted of four rooms enclosed by the screened veranda Papa had promised. Smudge pots and torches provided an additional defense against mosquitoes for the evenings when they were the worst. Through the trees Homer and I caught glimpses of a farm, a sawmill and the camp for the workers, but for the time being we could not think of exploring. Mama spent the whole rest of the day unpacking and arranging furniture to her satisfaction, and she found plenty of jobs for us.

When night came, we were delighted to learn we were to sleep in hammocks on the veranda. We went eagerly to bed, not with the idea of sleeping, naturally, but merely to try out the hammocks. We climbed in and out of them several times and rocked back and forth to learn how hard we could swing before provoking a shout of "Cut that out!" from inside the house. Finally, we dozed off, but it was not for long.

"E-E-E-E-E-E-E-A-A-H."

We were suddenly awakened by a horrible scream from out in the swamp. It seemed like it would take the roof right off the veranda above our heads. Before it had died away, Homer and I were both out of our hammocks and in bed with our older bothers and sisters.

The scream had awakened Mama, too. I could hear her in the next room. "William, what was that?" she asked in a strained voice, indignant as much as scared.

I held my breath, listening for Papa's answer.

"A cat, Emma."

"What kind of a cat?"

"A wildcat. A panther. They live out in the swamp. They won't come in the house."

"Does that infernal din go on every night?"

"No, but Big Jack says it'll get worse when they're mating. There's alligators, too. They don't scream. They bellow. I told you this was going to be no pleasure trip down here."

"Oh."

That was all Mama said, but I knew what she was thinking. She had found a reason to hate Florida that was sure to wear better and last longer than the mosquitoes, the snakes and the sticky heat combined.

Next morning in the daylight, Homer and I forgot how scared we had been. We would not even have minded seeing one of the wildcats - - from a safe distance. As soon as we could get away, we were off to explore.

Between the house and the construction camp was a small farm which provided fresh vegetables, eggs and dairy products for the camp. We saw several men working there but did not stop to make their acquaintance. Farming was already familiar to us. It was the work on the drainage project that we were eager to learn about.

Though the worker's camp was only a short distance from the house, Homer and I had been forbidden to go there. According to Mama, the men were all a rough lot whether black or white, and it was dangerous for us to associate with them. Naturally, this warning only increased our curiosity about the camp, and we poked into every corner of it. We investigated storerooms, a kitchen big enough to cook for all one hundred workers, and the tents for the men where they slept in deep piles of Spanish moss, without pillows or blankets. Everywhere we went, the men made us feel welcome. We saw no sign of the danger Mama had talked about.

In the blacksmith shop we found Big Jack at work and sat down to talk with him. He answered our questions about Florida patiently and filled the swampland around the camp with dangers more real than any Mama had brought to our attention. He told us about alligators, cotton mouths, coil snakes, hoop snakes, panthers, rattlers and a little green snake that curled inside the Spanish moss. Snapping cooters, the big dry land tortoises were another thing to watch out for. They dug holes and backed into them, leaving just their heads sticking out. They would take a hunk out of whatever happened by, just to see if it was tasty. It seemed like most everything in Florida was laying in wait for something to happen by.

Big Jack also talked to us about sand fleas and sand spurs, but we had already made their acquaintance, so we did not listen closely. Sand fleas were like our dog fleas, only they preferred to bite people. Sand spurs had a painful thorn that stuck fast in the feet of anyone who walked over them barefoot, as we had learned first hand. By the time we left the blacksmith shop to go home, we felt better prepared to deal with the perils of our new life. At least, we had an idea of what to avoid and where it was found.

As days came and went, Homer and I grew to love the wild lonely place where Papa's work had brought us. We were free here, unhampered except by natural boundaries we could understand. The twins were happy anywhere there was food and love, and the other members of the family gradually got to where they could tolerate life at the drainage project, since there was nothing better to be had anyway. Mama, however, went right on finding reasons to dislike Florida, and she did not keep them to herself. She was constantly complaining about how hard her life was in comparison to her sisters'. Finally, Papa had enough of it. He turned on her in anger in the presence of the whole family, a thing he very seldom did.

"Emma! I am the head of this house, and you are my wife. I love you and I love my children, and I do my best to provide for you and them. You were the one who insisted on coming with me. Now, you're here, and I'll hear no more of your nagging and complaining. If I do, we will continue to live here after this job is completed. We won't go back to Arkansas, and that is a promise. Now, you go about the business of making this place a home like I know you can, and shut up!"

Without waiting for Mama's reaction, Papa got up and headed for the door. Striding past me, he stopped briefly to place his hand on my head a moment, as if he knew who would get the brunt of what was coming and wanted to apologize for it. Then, he was gone.

Mama sniffed and blew her nose. With a swirl of skirts, she grabbed the broom. "Well, you heard the . . . the . . . the . . . the . . . Oh! Get busy!"

I bent to pick up a nest of Spanish moss in which we had kept a young bunny, but I was not fast enough. Mama swatted me with the broom across the behind, and I went headfirst into a box of dishes. But for the quick action of Homer, the whole box would have crashed.

"Get out of here!" Mama screamed at me. "Can't you ever do anything right?"

"But it was your doing," protested two of the older girls at once.

That was too much for Mama to bear. She ran from the room to relieve her pent-up self pity alone and without sympathy. The rest of us went about our chores quietly. We had no desire to provoke another outburst.

Papa remained at the outer camp for four days. When he returned, Mama was as sweet and kindly spoken as she could be. We did not hear everything that passed between them, but that weekend, they took the big car and went to Tallahassee.

Homer and I watched from the veranda as the car pulled out of the yard and onto the road along the drainage Canal. "Betcha she ain't gonna like Florida no better when she gets back," said Homer. "She' gonna get mad at everything, and we're gonna catch it some more. We gotta find us some friends. Then, when Mama's looking for somebody to give a licking to, we'll have someplace to go to get out of her way."

"Who you think we night be friends with," I asked. I had no objection to my brothers plan, but I knew none of the men in the construction camp had their families with them.

Homer thought a moment. "Well he said, "there's a house on the way to town, the Knights, and when we went by there, I saw a boy and girl about our size hanging on the gate. We could go down there and ask to borrow a cup of lard. Everybody's got lard, and we could get acquainted like that. Ellie won't care if we're gone a while."

We were soon crossing through a patch of eggplants on the way to the Knights'. I had one of Mama's china cups for the lard we intended to borrow. Homer carried a poker in case we saw any snakes. I was terribly afraid we might see one and held tight to Homer's hand the whole way, but nothing hissed at us or came slithering out of the brush.

As we approached the Knights', a big dog, mangy and fierce looking, started barking and dashed madly at the picket fence surrounding the house as though trying to get at us. He alerted the family that we had arrived. It being Sunday, they were all at home and came out onto the sagging front porch. There was an old man, a woman of indeterminate age, and the two children. The porch looked about to collapse under their combined weight. We stood our ground outside the fence.

"Shut up, Boll!" yelled the old man, and the dog slunk into a favorite spot under the creaking porch. That accomplished, the old man spat tobacco. "You uns want sumpin?" he asked, grinning at us as if we were a huge joke.

Homer took the cup from me and held it out. "Can you all loan us a little lard?" he asked.

The old man spat again, then answered. "Wall, now, ain't that sumpin? Mighty folks gits low on vittles same as poor folk like us uns. Come in. Come in."

We untied the rawhide string that held the gate, walked in and handed the cup to the old man. He took it and inspected it, then handed it without a word to the woman by his side. She took it in her hands, held it close and ran her calloused fingers over the rose pained on the side.

"My, my, ain't that nice now," she said, trying to talk around a snuff brush held in one side of her mouth. She smiled at us. "Jes a minny. I'll go fer to git some of my nice fresh turtle fat. Jes made and hit's real tasty."

As the woman disappeared into the house for her turtle fat, the boy and girl sidled over to where we stood. They were about our ages and nut-brown from the sun. Their hair stood wild and unkempt, but they smiled at us. The girl squinted one eye at us and said, "If'n you uns wanna play sometime, us can meetchas at the water tower. Can't go no fudder. You all is too uppity and citified."

"Ain't neither," protested Homer. "We just plain people. Ain't nothing uppity 'bout us, and we left all our friends back home where we come from. We just lonesome and want someone to play with."

While my brother was speaking, I nodded and kept slapping mosquitoes right and left. My neck was a mass of lumps.

The old man noticed my plight. "Willie," he finally said the girl. "Git some of your maw's myrtle and give that gal. Look to me she don't know ol' skeeter don't like ol' myrtle no how."

The girl ran into the house and came back with a handful of leaves which the old man crushed in his hands. He jumped down from the porch, grabbed me and started rubbing my arms, legs and neck. "Skinny, ain't you?" he said.

Homer was scared for me. He almost used the poker on the old man before he realized what was going on, but he remembered in time about the man who helped us out on our trip down from Arkansas and came over for a share of myrtle.

We had noticed a greenish tint to the skin of people in the swamps before, and now we learned the secret of it. Juice from the myrtle leaves turned our faces and hands green, but it also got rid of the mosquitoes like a miracle, and this time we knew what it was so we could gather it ourselves. We thanked the old man and told him Mama would be thankful, too.

"Warn't nothing," he said, but he was pleased.

The woman came back now, bringing us the turtle fat, but we did not leave right away. We stood around in the yard talking. Child-like, we answered all their questions frankly, and they answered ours. They were as curious about us as we were about them.

When we left to go home, we had a sense of accomplishment. We had new friends with the Knight children, Willie and Sathe, and we had learned about crushed myrtle leaves keeping off the mosquitoes. Of course, we also had the turtle fat, but that was not an accomplishment. It had a peculiar smell.

"What you reckon we ought to do with it?" I asked.

Homer was prompt with the answer. "Throw it out and wash the cup good with lye soap. Mama ain't gonna want none of that in the house, even when she's in Tallahassee."

Mama was delighted to learn about the wax-leaf myrtle when she got home. We had to give thanks for it at prayer time every evening from then on. Other things were added to the prayer list as we found out about them from Willie and Sathe.

Spiderwort was good for the easement of pain whether from cuts, bruises or blisters. Saw palmetto was useful in building things, and the heart of the stalk could be eaten raw for food. Dasheens, or elephant ears, had thick roots which could be baked like potatoes or boiled in stews, and sparkle berry was a thirst quenching source of quick energy.

Homer and I sampled many of these new foods, but we drew a line at frog eggs fished out of the sloughs. We also developed a different notion of eggplant than we had had before. People in Florida cooked eggplant with every kind of meat imaginable. It went into the stew with rabbit, with chicken, with turtle or with squirrel, and we ate it until we never wanted to see another of the purple things.

Playing with our new friends, Homer and I began to get an idea of how people lived in the swamps. Many preferred to live off the natural provisions of the land rather than work a field or garden. For meat they caught crawfish, turtles, armadillos, frogs, rabbits, ducks and other wild game. Fruits grew profusely; pawpaws, mangoes, wild grapes, berries of all kinds, tangerines, peaches and citrus fruit.

There was no excuse for anyone to go hungry winter or summer. The only problem was preservation of food without ice or refrigeration. Food could be canned or dried, but the canning was limited because of a lack of containers and proper sealers. Beeswax was sometimes used, or salt or a heavy coat of lard.

We did not dare ask too many direct questions about the people who lived in the swamps, but by listening to Willie and Sathe, we gradually learned about our neighbors. All the menfolk were white, and the women were mostly Indian, mulatto or Cuban. Some were a mixture of English and Irish, pretty much like ourselves. We thought we had met everybody for miles around, heard of them at least, but we were wrong. One day Willie happened to mention a family who lived deep in the swamp.

"You ever go out there?" I asked with interest.

"Oh, no!" Willie was horrified. "Pa'd skin us'n. They got the evil eye."

Homer and I looked at each other doubtfully, uncertain what she meant.

"You know," persisted Willie. "If'n you catch them looking at you, you jes natural like follow them into the swamp, and you never leave again. They live in the ol' Langford house. Oak Stump Sam is the ol' man that's the head of all of them. He was a hangman up north one't but then he went stone raving mad after a hanging when he found out he hanged his very own brother. That's when he cum down here. He got three growed up boys, Pony Joe, Bull-in-a-Pen and Willard."

"Willard the Turtle," added Sathe. "Anybody know him far as they can see him cummin'. He walk real slow and push his head in and out, in and out, jes like ol' turtle."

These fascinating details only increased my curiosity to see the house and the people. I resolved to go. Homer was less enthusiastic, but he did not feel right about letting me go by myself. Willie and Sathe were quite reluctant, but they hated being left out, and a little danger was fun when there were four of us to share it. They agreed to guide us out to the place the following afternoon.

There was no road out to the Langford house. Homer and I would never have found our way without a guide. We had no idea we were anywhere near the place when Willie and Sathe stopped suddenly. "It's jes up ahead," whispered Willie, "but you can't see it good less'n you git up on this knoll and climb up them sycamores."

Homer and I nodded.

Soon, we were looking at the house from the lower branches of a sycamore tree. It was a huge place which could only have been built by some freak vision of future prosperity that never came true. Now, it was crumbled and windowless, covered with a thick growth of wild honeysuckle and morning glory vines. It sagged and seemed to sway in the wind. Something moved on the porch, whether animal or human being we could not tell. Then, all was quiet.

"You really goin' down there?" asked Willie.

"Sure," I said. I did not tell Willie, but I had Blue's turtle bone in my pocket, so I felt more or less protected. I also knew a few words to ward off spells though I had not tried them against the evil eye.

"Don't worry," said Homer, meaning to reassure both Willie and me. "If they hurt you, I'll run for Papa. Willie and Sathe can stay here hid to see what they do with you."

I nodded and started down the hill toward the house. Though I was not really scared, I felt in the pocket of my pinafore for the turtle bone, then reached deeper for a present I planned to give Mrs. Oak Stump. It was a pin from Mama's dresser, one she seldom wore and probably would not miss. It was set with shiny green stones, all but one vacant place where a stone had fallen out. Taking the pin in my hand, I sauntered up to the overgrown porch and hallowed in a louder voice than I would have thought possible for me.

"Mrs. Oak Stump!"

No one answered. No one appeared. A barn swallow rushed out through a paneless window in the front of the house and scared me almost out of my wits. I gathered up my courage and hallowed again. "Mrs. Oak Stump Sam!"

This time, a voice from the side of the porch asked, "What in tarnation air ye a-squawking 'bout gal. What ye want?"

A young man with bright red hair came out from behind a decayed pillar of the porch. He was loose-lipped in a rather half-witted way. His sad eyes looked me up and down, but there was nothing evil about them I could see. I smiled at him and said politely, "Is your mama hereabouts?"

"Silly's hereabouts," he said slowly. "Ye Uns want sumpin, better ye talk at Silly." He raised his voice to carry into the house. "Silly! Cum-a-runnin'!" From the way his voice echoed, the house was apparently empty.

A woman appeared suddenly as if from nowhere. She stood firmly before me, feet flat on the floor. The garment she wore had once been red, and before she put on weight it had probably fit. Now, it clung tightly to her not too unshapely body, greasy and spotted with dirt.

"Why ye cum here?" she asked. "Better git, chile, 'fore my ol' man git home."

"This yourn?" I asked. I held the pin out so the sun could reflect its rays through the glass stones.

The woman stood looking at it hypnotized and reached out hesitantly to touch it. "Guess not," she said, drawing her hand away. "Mine didn't have no stone missin'."

I knew she had been tempted. "Maybe the stone fell out," I suggested. "You reckon?"

The eager look in her eyes was something I understood. "It might be, gal. It jes might be. Cum in and sit a spell."

"Well, just fore a minute."

The woman cast a look at the half-witted boy. He grinned and sidled over to where we were and was told to bring a bucket of fresh water. He scampered away, chuckling to himself.

Inside the house were several other women, all unkempt like Silly. They seemed hungry for a chance to talk with someone from outside their own circle and gathered around to admire the pin. The happy look on their faces was a pleasure to see. Silly gave me a smile as she pinned the bauble I had given her on her faded and stained red dress.

We talked some after that. They told about their life in the swamp, and I told about Papa being a civil engineer on the drainage project. Finally, I said I had to go. I knew Homer and the others would be worried about me. The women were sorry to have me leave.

"Ye un cum again," invited Silly.

I promised I would.

Back on the knoll under the sycamores, Willie and Sathe were amazed at Silly's invitation when I told them about it. They said Oak Stump Sam's people kept very much to themselves and had never let anyone else come around before. All the way home they thought about it but decided they had best not go on account of the licking their father would give them if he ever found out.

Homer and I went alone on our subsequent visits to the old house in the swamps. We always found a welcome from Silly and the other women. They used only a few of the rooms on the ground floor, the kitchen, the pantry and several bedrooms. The rest of the house was vacant, and Homer and I were free to play anywhere in it we liked. The rooms reeked of decay, old rugs and fungus. Mushrooms grew in odd corners. If we broke anything, it went unnoticed. After the way Mama kept house, that was a great attraction for Homer and me.

We never saw the menfolk. At first, the women would not even talk about them, but gradually they learned to trust us. One day we told about our experience with the chain gang, and after that they were less reluctant to talk. Several of their men had escaped from the chain gang, which was why they spent their days deep in the swamp, trapping, smuggling and making home-brew as we figured out from bits and pieces Silly told us. It did not matter to us. After what we had seen of our cousin Luke Feaster, we would not have turned anybody into the chain gang, no matter what they had done.

One morning when we went to the Langford house, Silly met us on the porch. "Got to be quit today," she said. "My man, he sick wi' fever and chills."

"You call a doctor?" asked Homer.

"Ain't no doctor this side Louisbourg," muttered Silly, "and he wouldn't cum out here no ways."

"Mama'd come," said Homer. "She's a nurse, and she knows 'bout as much as a doctor. She was always taking care of sick folks at home in Arkansas and birthing babies, too."

"You think she cum?" asked Silly hesitantly.

"Sure," we said in one breath and took off running for our house.

Homer and I made the distance home in record time and burst onto the veranda where Mama was sitting. Homer started talking as we came up the steps. "They tol' us they can't pay a doctor to come all the way out to the swamp, and anyways they said a doctor wouldn't come to treat the likes of them."

"Who?" asked Mama.

"Them people out at the Langford house."

"Where?"

"We'll show you."

Mama got out of her chair instantly and went to get her nursing things. I congratulated Homer with a smile and a wink. The mere thought that a doctor might put money ahead of treating the sick was enough to make Mama furious. She would go straight out to the Langford house and never stop to think how we had make the acquaintance of people like that, much less punish us for it.

Silly was relieved to see the three of us come. She took us right in to where her husband was. Mama sent straight to work. She was familiar with malarial fever and knew how to make a sick person feel at ease. Whatever her other faults, she was a born nurse.

To Mama's delight, the man was strong and well-built, very handsome as well. He had a way with him. It was soon apparent that he and Mama were a match for each other. After the first relax of shaking, she said authoritatively, "Now, Mr. Oak Stump Sam - - a sturdy name, I must say - - if you will follow my advice, I can help you. If you won't, then God help you, for I know the signs, and you have the fever."

Shaking like a palm leaf in a hurricane wind, he shivered out, "Do yer dirt, woman. Can't you see I'm a sick man? If you got a spell, let her rip."

Mama started the women folk to boiling their drinking water. She told them the water they had been drinking, plus the mosquitoes, could get a person down quick. Since she talked in what was to them an outlandish language, they were a little bit afraid, but I helped to ease them over their first distrust by telling them how she had treated Papa and the men at the "works." I stretched it a little, but they soon accepted Mama's words as a sort of witch doctor spell.

Mama brewed some sassafras tea and dug into her supply of quinine with aspirin powder. She used paregoric to relax the man. He was so thankful by that time, and so infatuated with Mama, that I think he was trying to figure out a way to prolong his illness even before he began to recover.

That was the beginning of a busy time for Mama. Word soon got around in the swamp, and people began to come to her for help. When the doctor in Leesburg heard about her, he made a special trip to our house to meet her. He was a conscientious man and glad to think the people around Okahumpka would have someone to turn to for medical help.

"Mrs. Crenshaw," he said, "any way that I can help you I will be just pleased to do it. I'll be frank with you. I have felt bad about not coming down here and treating these folks more than I do, but you've seen that road from Leesburg, and you know yourself that anybody who really needed a doctor would most likely be dead before I could get down here and give them some help."

With the official backing of the doctor, Mama again assumed a position of importance. She had missed the contact which people nursing brought her and was as happy to be meeting people again as our neighbors were to have help with their illnesses. Though Mama did not lose her dislike of Florida, she at least had something else to occupy her mind.

Life smoothed out for Homer and me. Mama was too busy with her work to find reasons for giving us lickings all the time. Our oldest sister had charge of us for the most part, and Elinor was happy enough to give us permission to get out of her sight. We were free to play with Willie and Sathe or visit the Langford house or fish all afternoon in the slough with a bent pin for a hook. We were free to love Florida to our heart's content.

CHAPTER XVII

Into the Swamp

Mama's nursing brought us into contact with the people who lived in the surrounding swamps, but it was our friendship with Willie and Sathe that really gave us a chance to understand them. They had their own beliefs about God and man, their own code of right and wrong, and their own ways of punishing the people who violated it. More astonishing to Homer and me was the fact that the offender seldom resisted his punishment. He or she seemed to feel that it was deserved. We saw the system in operation at close range one day when we went on an excursion with Willie and Sathe.

We went to Bug Springs, a very deep spring with clear cold water, located near town. Homer and I had already visited it during the weeks we lived in the hotel, but at that time no one had thought to tell us about ol' man Dunwood's mules. According to Willie, Mr. Dunwood had driven to the spring with a wagon load of barrels, meaning to get some water. He had backed up to the spring and set the brake, but somehow the wagon had started rolling down the slope, dragging the mules with it into the water. They were there now on the bottom of the spring, the mules still in their harness, and you could see them through the clear water if you looked hard enough.

Apparently, Homer and I did not look hard enough, for we saw no sign of the mules or the wagon, but coming away from the spring we saw something else of almost equal interest. There was a girl about Ellie's age approaching the spring, and at the sight of her, Willie cupped her hand around her mouth and started talking to Homer and me in an urgent whisper.

"That Liddy Skaggs, she done been diddling aroun' with one of them outlanders, and she done got herself in the family way. She gettin' pointed at."

"Same like anybody else gits pointed at," said Willie, not realizing how complete our ignorance was on the subject. She pointed her finger at the approaching Liddy and encouraged us to do the same. "Go on. Point your finger."

I did so, feeling a little guilty about it. The poor girl dropped her head and slunk past us, keeping as far to one side as the path would allow. I was amazed that the gesture should have such a prompt and visible effect. We questioned Willie and Sathe about it on the way home.

"Many folks git pointed at hereabouts?" asked Homer.

"Pa done told us 'bout lots," said Willie.

"Yeah," agreed Sathe with obvious reservations, "but we ain't never seen but one."

"Scaley Haley."

"He's an uncle of ourn," said Willie. "The way he told it, a bee stung him in the privy and when he cum runnin' out, his pants fell, but Pa says that warn't no cause fur a growed man to run naked aroun' whar thar was womenfolk. He ain't held his head up since folks started pointing at him. Maw says he pining away. Sits all the time in an ol' rocker on his porch and don't hardly talk to nobody."

"Is folks still pointing at him?" I asked.

"Yeah."

"How long do they do it for?"

Willie and Sathe looked at each other. It was clear the question had not occurred to them before. "Long as they reckon they ought to," said Willie, and Sathe nodded.

After that, whenever Homer and I had a chance, we watched to see what went on. We did not see Scaley Haley much, so we could not tell if he was pinning away or not, but we saw Liddy Skaggs almost every time we were in town and knew for ourselves what was happening. Every time she came in sight someone pointed at her. They never accused, never said a word, just pointed, but it was enough. I could feel what a dreadful punishment it was to be set apart from everyone else like that, and I surely felt sorry for Liddy.

Pointing at people was not the only thing that surprised Homer and me about the way of life in Florida, but there were many things about our way of life which surprised Willie and Sathe, too, so we were even, more or less. The screens Papa used to enclose our veranda were a wonder, not only to our playmates but to the whole country around Okahumpka. People traveled out of their way to have a look at them, especially after Mama's nursing provided a natural excuse to come. The fact that we had domestic animals for meat instead of living off the land was also considered a bit peculiar by our neighbors and got us the name of being citified, but the general interest in our doings reached a high point when Papa grew alarmed about the condition of our animals and introduced sheep dipping.

Florida's abundant insect life was as troublesome for sheep, cattle and horses as it was for people. Fleas, stick-tights, ticks, flies and screw-worms all took their toll of the defenseless animals. There was no fence around our pasture, so the cows wandered pretty much where they liked in search of feed. They came back covered with parasites of every kind.

Dipping cattle had just become a new government project, and Papa made it welcome in Okahumpka. With the help of the U.S. Department of Agriculture, he built vats through which people could drive their cattle, fenced the surrounding area and hauled the dipping solution from the station. When all was in readiness, he announced a date for the first public dipping.

We were the only people who showed up that first time. Papa came down with the men who did the farming at the construction camp and gave instructions about what to do. While some of the men guided the cattle into the vats, others held the animals' heads out of the creosote solution as they were driven through. A third group skimmed the accumulated mass of pests from the top of the vat and brought it over to a fire to be burned. The dead insects popped and crackled in the flames. Homer and I had the job of keeping that fire going, and we smelled of burning pests and creosote for days afterward.

The people in the swamps were slow to accept any new idea, but when they saw that our animals survived the dipping and the ticks did not, they began to bring their own cattle, sheep, dogs and cats as well. When the animals emerged from the vat, most were turned loose to find their way home, and their owners were free to stay and chat with friends and neighbors as long as they wished. Only people who lived at a distance drove their animals home for fear they might get lost.

Dipping day became a kind of holiday, a reason for people from all over to get together, and with so many people bringing animals, the dipping was a dawn to dark operation. Women brought basket lunches, while the men cooked turtle soup or barbequed piglet, wild, to be sure, but tasty. The picnic grounds were near the water tower, well away from the dipping vats, a necessary precaution in view of the odor from the fire where the skimmings were burned.

Life went on at the dipping grounds in every sense. One young woman had her baby during the dipping, and folks promptly named it Little Dipper. Another day, an old lady died of "chess pains." The family put her in the back of a wagon, threw a tarp over her and went on with the activities of the day. "Hit's her time to go," said her daughter calmly. "She done been wantin' to fur a long time. No fun lef' fur her, she say, now, she's gone shore's anything."

Homer and I always managed to be at the center of whatever went on at the dipping grounds, but we seldom had more to see and do than the day Oak Stump Sam's people brought their animals to be dipped. They had a regular menagerie; two milk goats, a billy goat, some hens, a scrawny, almost featherless rooster, a flock of geese, two lean hounds and a bobcat they had caught and raised from a kitten. It took the half-witted boy to handle the bobcat. They seemed to have something in common. The cat spit a little at first, but he let the boy pick him up and put him in the vat. When the boy let go of him, he took off swimming like a paddling dog. When he got out of the vat, he shook like one, too - - all over everything.

Possibly to get us out from under foot at the dipping, Papa gave us a tent like those used at the construction site, for a playhouse. Willie, Sathe, Homer and I furnished it with crates and piles of Spanish moss, but we felt we needed other things to make it complete. All we had for kitchen stuff was a cracked dish and a fork with broken tines. It was Willie who thought of the solution for our problem. She remembered her pa telling about an abandoned shack in the swamp behind their house, and we decided to go and look for it on the chance that there might be something in it we could use.

The weather for our excursion was typical Florida, hot and sticky. Homer and Sathe found a machete and sharpened it at the blacksmith shop with some help from Big Jack. Willie and I had cane knives.

We started out eager and excited. But within the first few hundred yards, we nearly frightened ourselves out of our wits with stories about people who became lost in the swamp and were never heard from again. We touched each other for support and fell silent, which was probably the best thing that could have happened. We almost entered a clearing where a wild hog and her litter and a couple of young boars with long tusks were devouring the carcass of some animal. It was lucky we had been silent and downwind.

To skirt the area, we had to wade in muck. Sathe picked me up and carried me on his shoulders. "Only thing heavy 'bout you is your eyes." he said. "They the biggest things 'bout you." When we stopped for a breather, however, he was puffing as he set me down on the stump of a log.

"Sure better be worth this God-awful trip," said Homer in disgust.

The rest of us gasped, and Sathe said, "God ain't gonna like that. You better make a cross quick, or we uns may lose our way."

Chagrined and a little worried, Homer drew the cross. We all said, "Please, God, forgive Homer. He was just hot and tired. He didn't mean it." When we looked up at each other, it was easy to see that we were all relieved.

At that moment, a huge snake slithered out from under the tree stump where I was sitting. He looked at us with open mouth, stuck out his tongue and disappeared into the underbrush. Willie was the first to recover her voice.

"That was the ol' devil himself," she whispered. "He was jes waitin'. If'n we hadn't asked God to forgive Homer, he would have lost us all in this ol' swamp!"

None of us disagreed with her.

A little further along, Homer and Sathe found a path by the side of a clear water branch. We followed the branch to a small spring and there was the shack. It was not a proper house at all, just a roof and three walls with one side completely open. We crowded and pushed up to the open side.

The man who built the place had used provisions at hand to fashion a shelter for himself. The shack was made of palmetto fronds intertwined with ivy and wild grapevine. The floor was packed hard, but a few of the vines had found looser earth near the wall and taken root. A fireplace of muck stone and sticks filled one end of the shack.

The dank smell of disuse and damp earth hung in the air. A pair of torn and faded overalls hung by one suspender from a peg, a tobacco tin still stuffed in the pocket. A black comb with half the teeth missing rested on a stone shelf. A piece of cloth of undetermined color or use was wadded in a corner, covered by mildew and spider webs. A tin plate, a two-tined fork and a few pine knots were arranged carefully by the fireplace as though waiting for their owner to return. Dirt and leaves covered them, almost completely.

We began poking around in the shack. There was a canvas bag against the back wall, and when Willie nudged it gently with her cane knife, it jangled. She dumped it on the dirt floor to see what was inside. A tintype picture of a very plump woman fell out, followed by a watch chain, an empty tobacco tin, a pair of cuff links, a moldy shirt with a stripe pattern in faded purple and several small items, among them a marble, a ring and a pipe.

"He done met Ol' Man Death," Willie said solemnly. "I jes bet he wouldn't go away and leave all this."

We all nodded in agreement.

Further searching revealed a ball and chain in the corner of the shack beside the fireplace. The chain had been sawed in two, apparently close to the ankle. Wanting to see if there was anything of interest in the fireplace itself, Homer took a long stick, evidently a poker from the way it was burned on one end, and used it to stir the wood and ashes. He found something right off. The tail of a rattlesnake reared out of the drifted leaves, shaking violently in warning. When Homer jerked the stick away, the snake hissed and disappeared through a hole in the crudely mortared stones.

"Feller that lived here's dead all right," said Homer. "Ol' snake bit him, and he run off in the swamp and died."

The rattlesnake dampened our enthusiasm for any further search of the shack, and we were soon headed for home. Willie chose the ring for her part of the treasure we had discovered. Sathe took the ball and chain, though we all took turns carrying them for him, so he would have both hands free to hack brush with the machete. Homer and I took the picture, the marble and the watch chain.

As far as furnishings for our tent was concerned, the trip was in vain. All we had to show for our efforts were the tin plate and the two-tined fork. The man who built the shack had been too poor to own any on the things we wanted.

The trip home was easier than the trip into the swamp had been. The way was blazed with lopped off branches and trampled grass, and we could concentrate on something besides where to put our feet next. Willie stopped suddenly, shushing the rest of us with her finger pressed against her lips.

"Ain't that a big ol' cooter up there?" she whispered and pointed to the path ahead.

She was right. As we watched, a large terrapin eased out onto the trail we had made. He was as big as a small wash tub. He poked his ugly head around taking in the situation, decided he had nothing to worry about and waddled on. We followed him quietly, the boys cut two stout poles. When we got close enough, Homer and Sathe pushed the poles under the cooter's body while Willie and I beat his head to make him keep it inside his shell. He could have bitten a fair sized piece out of one of us if he had gotten a good hold.

When the boys had the cooter firmly settled on the poles with his back legs hanging over one and his front legs over the other, they picked him up, and we set off for home. Willie and I took turns walking beside the cooter, and every time it looked as if he might stick his head out, we gave him another whack to make him pull it in. We carried him straight to the construction camp.

Several of the cooks were sitting on the steps of the mess tent as we approached. When they saw the cooter, they offered us a dollar for him. That was more than we had expected, but we knew better than to act surprised. It was a big terrapin, and the meat was tastier than turtle since the cooter ate roots instead of pond weed. Besides, the shell would also be valuable for a wash pan or a watering trough. We waited expectantly as the men dug into their pockets for the nickels, quarters and dimes to pay us.

Back at our tent, Sathe held his quarter in the palm of his hand studying it. "Ain't never had that much money at one time before," he said. "Not that was my own."

"What you reckon you gonna spend it for?" asked Homer.

Sathe shrugged. "Don't know. Might not spend it right away. When you go in town and see sumpin you like, hit's jes a nice feeling to know you could buy it, even if you don't. Once you spend money, hit's gone."

Homer, Willie and I nodded. We knew that was true about money.

I understood how Sathe felt about his quarter, because my twenty-five cents gave me a sense of security, but the marble I had chosen as my share of the treasure gave me a good feeling, too. The marble was neither very big or completely round, but it was smooth and cool to the touch. I planned to polish it and paste it on top of a cigar box I had.

When Papa saw it, however, he thought it did not look like a marble and suggested that we find out for sure what it was. He took it to a jeweler and learned that it was a pearl, quite valuable. The jeweler made a ring setting for it.

I glowed with pride the day that ring came home from the jeweler's in a tiny box and Papa and I presented it to Mama. She gave me a pat on the head and a real smile, one that was proud and happy, and promised that I would have the ring when I grew up. It was a great day for me. I had done something Mama approved of - - for once.

Chapter XVIII

Ole Gator

Papa's work on the drainage project remained somewhat of a mystery to Homer and Me, for we did not have many opportunities to watch what he did. His work often took him to outlying camps where we could not go. Furthermore, it involved dynamite, and we were forbidden to get anywhere near the site of the blasting. When the men began working on the lake near our house, however, the temptation was too much to resist. With Willie and Sathe, we found a hiding place behind some trees and watched the men at work.

Papa rowed himself out in a small boat to plant the sticks of dynamite. Big Jack and three other men held one end of a rope fastened securely to Papa's boat. As soon as he signaled that he had lit the fuse, they hauled him to shore, hand over hand, as fast as they could.

The explosions of dynamite were a terrifying thrill. Fish, snakes, alligators, turtles, frogs, mud and rotting vegetation flew into the air, and waves beat against the shore of the lake. When the blasting was over, some of the men went out with gunny sacks and gathered the fish which were floating on the surface of the water.

The lakes had always held an attraction for us, but after the dynamiting, they became the scene of all our most exciting imaginary adventures. We had been strictly forbidden to go near the lakes, but that did not keep us from pretending to captain ships and search for buried treasure. In fact, the only thing that held us back from some real adventures was our lack of a boat.

We prayed for a boat, and our prayers were finally answered, though by whom I am not sure. Homer and I found an old flat boat partly buried in the mud and swamp grass along the lake, and Willie and Sathe were soon at work helping to fix it up. The boys waded out into the shallow water and pushed and pried at the boat until Willie and I could wedge a prop under it to keep it from sliding back into the lake. With much heaving and shoving, the four of us succeeded in dragging the boat out on dry land and flopping it over against a log. It was a mess, with muck and rotting weeds trailing everywhere, but we were thrilled with it. We thought it was beautiful.

Willie and I scraped the bottom with pieces of glass and a broken iron hoop to remove the thickest of the mud. Then, Homer "borrowed two of Mama's precious shuck brushes, and we took turns scrubbing until the boat was clean. When it was dry, we chinked the cracks with pine resin, sweet gum and sheep's wool. For a final touch, the four of us gathered sour dock berries, mashed them and poured the juice into a small cooter shell. With this juice and Spanish moss for brushes, we painted the boat a beautiful dried blood color. We were proud of ourselves when we finished and could admire the results of our work. We thought ourselves smart.

"Ain't she purty tho'." said Willie.

"Shore is," agreed Sathe. "Reckon maybe we ought to float her now?"

"Nah," said Homer reluctantly. "It's getting late. Mama'll be 'specting us for dinner 'fore long, and tomorrow's Sunday, so we gotta go to church in the morning. Reckon tomorrow afternoon is the earliest we could do it."

Sathe nodded. "Yeah. That's the best idea. Then we uns can all pray in church that she don't leak."

Homer and I promised we would do that.

The promise was one we knew we would be able to keep, for Mama made sure that we attended church every Sunday. She was not about to let the swamp claim us completely, though we might not have minded that. Getting our whole family to church required great ingenuity, but Mama's skill as a manager was equal to the task.

Since we owned a car, Mama could not stand the thought of using any other conveyance for the weekly trip to church. The Model T, however, would not carry all of us, and that was where Mama's managing had its chance to work. She and the twins rode in the car, with Papa, Cal or Charlie driving. The rest of us walked, carrying our shoes in our hands so they would not get dirty. The car would go ahead until the sand got too much. We would catch up at that point and push until the car was out of the sand.

The Sunday of our boat launching was neither better nor worse than usual. In spite of the corduroy road, the car got stuck in sandbars a number of times and had to be pushed out. Mama waited for us where the hard road began near town, and all who could find a strap or brace to hang onto stayed with the car the rest of the way. A few still had to walk, so Mama waited again at a shady corner near the church ground.

"Why didn't you go on in, Maw?" asked Charlie for about the thirtieth time as he, Anna and Cal walked up.

"A family should attend church together," said Mama with a smile that was pleasant but firm. It was the answer she gave every Sunday. As we all entered the church ground, some riding and some walking, Mama once again satisfied herself that she had arrived in style.

In church, Homer and I kept our promise to Willie and Sathe. When the minister invited us to open our hearts to god in prayer, we bowed our heads and prayed that our boat would not leak and that our forbidden trip on the lake would be a success, just the beginning of high adventure. That done, church had no further interest for us. We were eager to start home.

Once home, my brother and I soon changed into play clothes and were off. We found our friends waiting for us at the boat. They were as excited as we were.

We decided to name our boat the "Sour Dock." Homer would be the captain, since he had found her, and he chose Sathe as his crew for the maiden voyage. Willie protested that she wanted to go too.

Sathe shook his head. "First we uns gotta find out if'n she leaks or not, and you can't swim real good."

That was the end of Willie's objections.

Tugging, rolling, lifting and swatting, we eventually got the "Sour Dock" into the lake. It fell in with a splash, and we all danced around, hollering and laughing. I suggested we should cover it with flowers of which there were thousands in the swamp. Quickly, we gathered oleander, wild orchids and honeysuckle. We made a wreath around the boat. The flowers floated gently on the water.

I had made a poem to sing for the launching;

Sour Dock, Sour Dock! Into the lake.

Look out ol' gator! Git away ol' snake!

We gonna ride the open waves.

Hunt for treasure, hunt for caves.

A cave would have been hard to find in the swamps, but I could not think of another word that fit. No one seemed to mind the inappropriateness.

"We gonna go all over these ol' lakes and swamps," said Willie. "We gonna show them ol' gators. Can't nothing like them scare us off."

We tied a long rope to the iron hoop in the bow, and our boat was ready to launch. With paddles laboriously made in the blacksmith shop at stolen moments. Homer and Sathe waded into the muck to push. When the water got up to our knees, we were sure the Sour

Dock was floating, and we were ecstatic. We whistled and splashed and threw flowers at each other.

The lake was not large, but to us it seemed like an ocean. While Homer and Sathe paddled out toward the middle, Willie and I watched from the shore, alert for any sign of trouble. I saw the dark shape on the water first. "Dynamite must have busted loose that ol' log floating out there," I said to Willie. "You reckon?"

Willie looked where I pointed and her eyes widened. "That ain't no log!" she said. "See? It's moving. That's a big ol' gator swimming, and he's headed for the boat."

Willie and I yelled a warning at the top of our lungs, but we could have saved our effort. Homer and Sathe must have seen the gator the same as we did, for they began heading to shore. They paddled furiously, but the boat did not seem to be moving very fast.

"Hurry!" screamed Willie.

"Can't," Sathe yelled back. "It's leaking and we ain't got nothing to bail with."

Willie and I looked at each other in terrified desperation. What could we do? With more good intentions than sense, we waded out through the water lilies and swamp grass to the edge of the shallows. Homer and Sathe were closer now, but so was the gator. The boys were poling the boat through the water lilies with the gator following them.

"They gonna make it!" whispered Willie.

Perhaps they would have, but at that moment the boat ran aground. There was nothing Homer could but throw us the end of the rope tied to the bow, and he was lucky to be close enough to

234

do that. Willie and I tugged with all our strength, but the boat was stuck fast. We sobbed and cried, but it was no help. The gator stuck his ugly snout up out of the water and opened his mouth.

Suddenly, we heard a crashing through the brush on the lake shore, and a series of shots whistled over our heads. The gator was hit. He bellowed with pain and rage and thrashed about until he finally flipped himself completely around and swam off. The air was full of the sickeningly sweet aroma of the water lilies he had crushed.

Slowly, we turned toward the shore. Big Jack was standing in the clearing where we had launched the boat. He crooked a finger at us. Homer and Sathe climbed out of the boat, meaning to help Willie and me pull it to shore, but Big Jack shook his head.

"You come on over heah. Now!" he said firmly. "And you jes as well leave that ol' boat be. You know, and I know that you ain't goin' out in it no more."

All four of us let go of the rope and waded to shore. We stood in a line in front of Big Jack, our shifts and pant legs dripping. We knew we had done wrong and were going to have to take the consequences, but we did not really mind. We were just glad Big Jack had been there. Something much worse than a mere licking might have been happening to us.

Big Jack shoved his pistol into his belt. He looked us up and down very slowly. "What yo' folks tell you 'bout them lakes?" he asked quietly.

"Stay off 'em," said Homer in a small voice.

"Why you reckon them to say that? You reckon they had a notion ol' gators was out there?"

All four of us nodded.

"Uh-huh!" confirmed Big Jack. "Don't doubt they did. By and by that lake gonna be safe. Them gators'll be dead, or they'll be tired of that dynamiting and looking for them some new homes. But, that lake ain't safe now. So, we got us two ways we can go. Firs', I tells yo' folks what you been doing down heah, and you gits lickings all 'round. Or second, I don't tell yo' folks, and you gonna promise me that you ain't goin' out on them lakes no more until yo' folks say you can. What you want? You reckon that second one's the bes' idea?"

We nodded again.

"All right. Hands out front. Ain't nobody crossing their fingers on me." Big Jack looked at Homer. "You goin' firs'?" he asked.

Homer took a deep breath. "I promise I ain't going out on the lakes no more unless Papa says I can."

Big Jack's gaze shifted to me. "I ain't neither," I said. "I promise."

"I ain't going." Willie said. "Cross my heart."

"You got my word," agreed Sathe in a voice the rest of us could barely hear.

He had been the closest to the gator, and he was still shook.

"Good enough," said Big Jack. "Mind you don't forget what you promised me."

On the way back to the house, Homer summed up what all of us were feeling. "We was lucky," he said. I nodded. We had been lucky- - in more ways than one.

We kept our promise to Big Jack faithfully, and he kept his to us. Mama and Papa never did find out about our escapade. When dynamiting was finished and the gators had been driven out, Papa let us go fishing on the lakes. It was fun, but it was safe too. The thrill of having a forbidden adventure was gone.

It was not only the adventure on the lakes that was over. The whole year-long adventure of our life in Florida was coming to an end. Drainage canals and ditches had been made, and the land between them was drying fast in the hot Florida sun. Homer and I were sad, but Mama was elated. She began packing for our return to Arkansas.

When Papa announced that we would be leaving in a couple of weeks, the word soon spread in the construction camp. Big Jack and several other men who had worked closely with Papa invited all of us to a sing at their church. There would be a dinner afterword, a time to say goodbye. Mama was delighted with the idea. It was one more tangible sign that she was really going to leave Florida.

Big Jack's church was a brownish-gray clapboard building put together with love and hard work. It had four windows, not all of which had panes. The pews consisted of half logs for the seats and boards nailed across the backs for backrests. The chairs where the choir sat were sawed logs cut crosswise to form stools. The lectern stood out against the simplicity of the other church furnishings. It was made from a beautiful, polished cypress stump, laboriously sanded and oiled, an offering from the faith of the people and their love of God which permeated the whole church.

As guests, we sat on a short log at one side of the regular pews. Brother Clopper officiated at the service. He could read and write, a fairly rare thing in the swamps, and he carried a Bible clutched close to his heart wherever he walked. It was plain to see everyone respected him. He was preacher, teacher, undertaker, doctor and general advisor. He stood up behind the lectern and began simply, "We gonna sing."

There were no books. None was needed. A lone fellow in the choir corner played a harmonica for accompaniment, and the songs literally poured out of that church. Ringing and reverberating, they must have loosened the boards. Voices of rare pitch carried notes so high I gasped for breath, while the bass notes were so low I felt myself drowning in their beauty. One way or another I think God's presence was truly felt by all. As Homer and I stood listening, tears streamed down our faces.

Brother Clopper presented a short, simple sermon. There was more singing afterward. Then, he asked for someone to pass a hat around.

"This is to get another window pane and a strip of carpet for the aisle," he said. "If you don't have money now, and many of us don't, just put a piece of paper in the hat for what you think you can give later on. I'll jot your name as I see you drop in the paper, and I'll be around to talk to you after a bit."

Ma Cain, a very fat woman, searched frantically and finally burst out with, "I'd like to do something on you' carpet, Brother Clopper, but I ain't got no paper."

Everyone laughed loud and long, friendly like.

Since some of the windows were open, wasps had been able to get in and build a nest in the ridge of the roof. While we were singing the last song, a boy took out his slingshot and made a perfect hit on that wasp nest, With screams and confusion, the church was cleared in a matter of minutes. When things had calmed down a little, the boy was led up to Brother Clopper to have judgment passed on him.

"While we all eat, Mistah Whit," said the preacher, "you gonna stay in the church with your conscience. Then when we done et all the good parts, you can come out and get you some of the leftovahs."

This was a real punishment, even though his mother softened it a bit by saving him some of the "good parts." There were a number of fine cooks in the group, and the food was delicious. Since we were guests, we had first choice of all the good things which embarrassed us a little, though Homer and I made full use of the opportunity. There were molasses cakes, pecan pies with pure cane syrup, eggplant so delicately flavored and crisp that even we were willing to try it. We discovered, however, that we could only eat so much.

After the meal, Brother Clopper presented each of us with a going-away gift from his congregation. I got a hand painted palmetto fan, Homer a palmetto hat. Mama got a fan and a special thank-you for the nursing she had done.

Speaking for all of us, Papa thanked the people for their invitation to the sing. He said he would get them the windows for their church and give them the screenwire from our porch when we left. Maybe it would keep the wasps out in the future. Everybody laughed at that.

Back home that night as Homer and I lay in our hammocks, I whispered to him through the darkness. "You know, I'm gonna miss all our Florida friends. Willie and Sathe. And Big Jack and Oak Stump Sam's people. In a way it's gonna be lonesome at home in Arkansas."

"Yeah," agreed Homer. "But there's Aunt Matt. She's our friend. And there's Blue. We can give him his turtle bone back and tell him 'bout everything we been doing down here. He'll be glad to know how much trouble that turtle bone kept us out of, I reckon."

I nodded at that. It was true.

Before we started for Arkansas, Papa stacked all the things we were not taking with us in one huge pile in the yard and told people to come help themselves if there was anything they could use. In less than an hour, nothing was left. We drove out of an empty yard on the way to Okahumpka where most of us would catch the train for home.

Chapter XIX

Papa goes to Jail

When we returned to Arkansas, we moved back into the same house with the same apple orchard and the same thirty-two steps leading up to the back porch, but somehow these familiar things had a different feel 'bout them. It was more then just the fact that a new church was being built nearby. Everything seemed to be slightly changed. Perhaps, our year in Florida had changed us in ways we did not completely understand.

Homer and I sensed that things were not going to be quite the same from the moment we got home, but a visit to Blue's was what really made us aware of the change. We wanted to surprise him with the news that we were back from Florida, so we hurried through the chores Mama assigned us and disappeared before she could discover we were finished and give us more unpacking and arranging to do. With the turtle bone safe in Homer's pocket, we cut across the fields, eager for the first glimpse of our friend's house.

Even from the road, the place had a different air about it than we had ever seen before. "Don't look to me like anybody's there," said Homer. "I wonder where they're at. It ain't Sunday or nothing."

He began to whistle "Ol' Dan Tucker" half-heartedly, but there was no sound from the house. No Blue came running out to meet us.

I tugged at Homer's sleeve. "There ain't no chickens, or no hound dogs, or nothing. You reckon they done moved and gone away?"

My brother and I stared at each other. It was a possibility we had never once considered until that moment. "Kinda looks that way, don't it?" said Homer. "One way to find out."

We walked through the arbor down the path to the front door and knocked. There was only a vacant sound in answer, and the door swung gently open when we pushed it. Inside, there were no dishes, no furniture, no picture of Jesus on the wall. The wooden rack over the fireplace where Popper Paradise had kept his gun was empty. The comics were still there, papering the wall on each side of the chimney. But neither Homer nor I felt any inclination to read them.

"They gone all right." said Homer, and the words echoed in the empty house.

We walked slowly back outside and climbed up on the fence around the pen which had belonged to Dooley Donkey. Sitting on the topmost board, we could look down to the creek where we had helped Blue build a pond for the ducks we gave him. We talked about him, wondering where he was and what he was doing and why he had moved away. We thought of the good times we had had with him, the tricks we had played on people and the spells he had taught us to keep us safe in Florida.

"Hey," said Homer suddenly, "Ain't that an ol' meadowlark singing down there in the pasture?"

I listened a moment. The bubbling song was unmistakable. "Sure is," I said. "Blue told us 'bout that 'fore we left. He said the meadowlark was gonna be from him to us, and it was gonna fly back to him fast as it could. You 'member."

Homer nodded. We smiled at each other and called out in unison, "Hi, Blue! Misses you."

"We was bringing your turtle bone back," added Homer. "It worked jes like you said. I reckon we'll keep it now, since you ain't here, but if you ever need it, we'll give it back, promise. All you gotta do is come 'round and ask."

"We sure do thank you for loaning it to us," I said. So the meadowlark would be able to tell Blue that Homer's promise was good for me as well.

Homer and I did not say much on the way home. I did not mention it to him, but I was thinking that trouble never came single. Everybody said so, Aunt Matt, Mama and Granny Paradise. So it must be true. I had even heard Willie say it once in Florida. Blue had moved away, our best friend, and that was trouble if anything was. I wondered what else was coming our way.

I kept on the lookout for the trouble that was coming, but nobody would have had the least difficulty recognizing it when it arrived. It came to everybody for miles around, more or less at the same time; diphtheria. The epidemic seeped slowly into our community, spreading like the Pearl River during the spring rains, not noticeable until it crept into your own yard.

As a nurse, Mama's help was constantly in demand, and she was one of the first people to realize how serious the situation might become. She isolated her own family immediately. We could not visit or have visitors. She boiled the water we drank, and hand washing with lye soap was an absolute must.

When she was called to attend the sick, Mama left explicit instructions for us all to follow during her absence, stressing that if we did not do as we were told she would be laying us out. She warned us that if anyone became ill, the sick person was to be placed in a back room she had prepared, and everyone else was to stay away from that room except Ellie. We were to fetch Mama from wherever she was immediately, using the buggy, not the car. The buggy was more reliable.

As the epidemic worsened, not a day passed that Mama was not called on to help with the seriously ill or lay out the dead. She appeared tireless. She came home for a change of clothes, a bath and a few hours of sleep. She would visit with the family, lay down a few laws, hold the twins awhile and be off to the next house where she was needed.

The twins had reached a stage of their life when everyone thought them cute. They babbled a lot and talked a little and were interested in everything that went on around them. Though Ellie took over most of their care, we all enjoyed helping her. One night when Mama was gone, we were horrified to be awakened by the raspy breathing of the boy.

"Maybe we're all gonna get sick now," whispered Anna. As we children held onto each other in fright.

When Ellie took charge, we did the chores and odd jobs she assigned us without fighting. Not knowing who might be the next to come down sick, we felt we should be nice to everyone while we had the chance. Papa gave Homer the responsibility of going after Mama in the buggy, and I went with him.

Mama was over five miles away at the Saunders' where the young son and maiden aunt had died. When we arrived, she knew immediately that someone was ill at home. All she said to Homer was, "Who?"

"It's Lewis, Mama," replied my brother. "Ellie says he's real bad."

I jumped into the back of the buggy. Mama grabbed the reins from Homer, and we were off, fairly flying down the road. We were home as fast as the horse could get us there, with Mama encouraging him all the way.

It was not fast enough. We realized we were too late when we saw the rest of the family gathered at the hitching rack to greet us. Ellie was beside herself. "I did everything you said, Mama," she wailed. "Everything!"

Mama just sat on the buggy seat for a moment. Then, she climbed slowly to the ground, and the tears began to come. "It's my fault," she sobbed with her head on Papa's shoulder. "I never should have left. I never should."

"There, Emma," Papa put his arms around her comfortingly. "You were needed, and you went."

Papa was suffering, too. I realized it just from the look on his face in the lantern light. He had nine girls and four boys, and to lose one of the boys was a sad thing. Indeed. Mama touched on that very point when she turned to go into the house. She swished around, looked us all over and said, "Why him, when we have so many girls?"

Papa jerked to life at that. "Are you questioning the hand of God, Emma?" he asked.

"No," said Mama after a moment's hesitation and went up to the house.

Papa headed for the barn to unhitch and tie up the horse. I followed him. When he leaned on the manger and wept, I stood close and hugged his leg. "Papa," I said, choking back my own tears, "I wish it was me. If I could, I'd be dead, and Lewis could be here."

Papa stopped crying then. He reached down to pick me up and set me on the back of the horse. "No, no, no, Ressie," he said, cupping my face in his strong hands. "I wouldn't want that. It wouldn't be any better than this. I love you just as much as I love Lewis."

Looking into Papa's eyes, I knew he meant every word, and I felt I could live on that assurance for weeks - - and - - months - - and even years.

Lewis' death convinced Mama that her precautions with lye soap and boiled water were not enough. She opened a campaign for inoculation, beginning with us. When we survived the treatment, she felt justified in carrying her message wherever she went in the community. The response was not always favorable, but Mama kept trying. It was her way of putting grief for Lewis behind her, making his death count for something.

"Those Mitchells!" began Mama one afternoon, returning from an especially discouraging visit. "They can just bury their own dead. They had a dozen reasons not to be inoculated, every last one of them superstition."

"Now, Emma," Papa soothed.

"Well, that's what it is."

A few evenings later, we were having a fireplace supper of chicken gruel and grits when there was a knock on the door, an occurrence by now familiar. Papa asked Homer to go see who it was, and of course I followed him. He opened the door, and there stood what looked like the ghost of Mrs. Mitchell. She was white, and tears ran down her cheeks in rivulets. Clinging to the door knob, she whispered "Your mother, is she here?"

"Come in, Mrs, Mitchell, please," I said. "Mama's resting." I took her hand and led her into the living room.

Papa and Cal jumped up to give her a chair, and one of the girls offered her a cup of soup. Weary from long hours of caring for her sick, she could scarcely hold the cup. She was nearly exhausted.

"It's my Savannah and Bryan," explained Mrs. Mitchell in a tired, hopeless voice. "Bryan's dead, and Savannah's dying, and I can't do nothing to help. Please, Mrs. Emma, can you come to our place again?"

"I'll go back with you just as soon as I can get my things together," said Mama, all nurse. "Sit right there and rest a minute while I get ready. I know how you feel. I lost one of my own. The Lord giveth and the Lord taketh away."

There was not a word said about inoculation.

While Mama gathered up her herbs and cures, Papa went out to the barn. The horse was used to such unexpected calls and responded as though he knew how important he was. Mama and Papa both went back with Mrs. Mitchell, Mama to do what nursing she could and Papa to measure the body for a casket.

Homer and I watched solemn-eyed the next morning as Papa made the coffin for Bryan Mitchell. Mama and Ellie worked on it also, padding it with carded cotton and lining it with white muslin, The rim was edged with lace, black lace.

Thus far in the course of the epidemic, Papa had already made several coffins out of lumber from his sawmill, for people like the Mitchells who wanted to bury their loved ones decently but were too poor to buy a coffin, especially at the prices Mr. Ashbury was asking in town. Many of the people who lived around us were sharecroppers, and before the fields were harvested, they were already in debt for the next years crop. They never saw cash money at all, so when a member of the family died, they needed the help of someone like Papa who would build a coffin for compassion's sake.

All this was natural to Homer and me. We watched Papa and Charlie load the latest coffin, Bryan Mitchell's onto the wagon and drive off down the lane. When they were out of sight, we thought no more about the matter.

That evening all of us were gathered around the fireplace, talking of this and that before prayers, when we heard a horse and buggy drive up outside. We waited for the expected knock at the door, but it did not come. Instead someone called out in a loud voice, "Hello, the house!"

Mama and Papa exchanged looks. "Sounds like young deputy sheriff Sparks," said Mama.

"Sure does," Papa agreed. Taking the lantern which was kept burning in the hallway for trips to the outhouse, he opened the front door and stepped out on the porch. "Light down and come in," he called.

Hillary Jupiter Sparks, better known as Jupe, jumped down from his buggy, tied the reins to the maple tree by the gate, and came up the path to the house. As he followed Papa into the room where we were all waiting for him, he looked uncomfortable but at the same time, aware of his own importance, and we were certain of the one thing right away. This was not just a neighborly call.

"Now Uncle Bill," began Jupe without looking at anybody directly. "I gotta do this, so's I sure don't want you to hold it agin' me. Myself, I think hit's a shame, but I ain't got no choice. Hit's the law. I gotta arrest you and take you to the jail house."

"What's that you're saying, Jupe?" asked Mama. "What are you babbling about?"

The deputy sheriff looked down at his feet. "Well, you see, Miz Crenshaw, Mr. Ashbury done . . ."

"Speak up, Jupe."

"Mr Ashbury has done sworn out a warrant agin' your husband. He claims you're taking business away from him 'cause you been making them coffins for these people out here, and you got your own business. Ain't nobody butting in on you. So's he done sent me out here to bring you in. Hit's the law now, Uncle Bill, ever since that Ol' Man Hammersill was most near in his grave when he done come alive. Now, the undertaker and the doc both gotta say when's a man dead, and the undertaker got a right to his own kinda business. You been making coffins right and left out here and helping bury the dead, and you jes ain't no undertaker nor nothing. See?"

"I see," said Papa.

"Well I don't," Mama interrupted, furious. "You can't send a person to jail for helping people that can't afford to bury their dead, Jupe Sparks! If you arrest my husband, you're gonna have to take me along with him because I lined the coffins and laid out the dead. Doc never told me they were dead, but I've got enough sense to know a dead one from a live one. That Ashbury is dead from his neck up. You just take William and me both in, and I'll have a few words to say to Judge Fitzpatrick when I get to his court."

"Now, Emma." Papa put a restraining hand on Mama's shoulder. "You've said more than a few words already. Just let it be." He turned to the deputy. "All right, Jupe. I'll go with you as soon as we've had our prayers. Will you join us?"

Jupe shuffled and turned red. His gun had never shot anything except maybe a rat or snake, and now it was in his way as he tried to kneel. He hitched the heavy belt around to a position which made kneeling possible and self-consciously joined the family.

250

I often felt that God must look forward to our family's prayer time, for he could learn so much of interest from it, and that evening was one of the most memorable. Mama started the prayers. She and God had quite a conversation about the need of a few people to show some love for their neighbors. Then Papa took over. By the time he had asked forgiveness for the sins committed for love of money, Jupe was feeling more and more ill at ease. Papa said his amen, followed by each of us in turn, in our regular pattern. We had all listened carefully to what was said to learn what was going on.

Mama was still outraged as she accompanied Papa and the sheriff to the door. "I'll be in town tomorrow and give that Ashbury a piece of my mind." she announced.

"No, you won't Emma," said Papa firmly. "You'll keep what mind you have. Mr. Ashbury wouldn't know what to do with a piece of it if you gave it to him. He evidently needs a whole mind. Don't worry. A man does what he has to do. I'll take care of things."

With that, he said goodnight to all of us and left with Jupe Sparks.

Mama ordered us right and left to vent her frustrations. Knowing what she was like in this mood, everybody was off to bed as soon as possible, and there under the covers we discussed the calamity in whispers. I cried myself to sleep, not so much for Papa who I knew could take care of himself, but for the people like the Mitchells who would now have no way to bury their dead.

I did not expect to see Papa again very soon, but he was back the following day. Jupe Sparks dropped him off at the end of our lane and drove on by without coming up to the house. He probably did not want to face Mama again.

"Well, William?" asked Mama, as Papa came inside.

"All taken care of," said Papa. "I'll deliver a load of my best red cedar lumber to Mr. Ashbury, and that'll square us for any money he feels he's been deprived of. Red cedar is premium lumber. If he don't want it for coffins, he can sell it easy enough."

"What happened at the courthouse?"

"You weren't needed, Emma." Papa chuckled. "The judge told Mr. Ashbury that if his fees were less, people might be more inclined to use his services. He suggested that if he was more charitable, he might look beyond the dollar sign and see that he was called on to bury people like the Mitchells whether they could pay or not."

I knew Judge Fitzpatrick was sensible," said Mama with an audible sniff. "If that Ashbury was to get any fee out of the Mitchells, he'd have to take the food they raised to live on. The cotton and cow peas go to the owner to pay for tilling and the rent on the farm house."

While the epidemic of diphtheria ran its course, Mama and Papa went right back to helping people however they could, which included building coffins. We had no further trouble with Mr. Ashbury, but even if we had, I doubt it would have kept Mama and Papa from acting as they did. They had their own notion of right and wrong, and helping wherever they could was part of it. Papa's day in court left only one permanent trace on their behavior. Mama joked forever afterward about being married to a desperado.

CHAPTER XX

The End of Childhood

I cannot really say when it was, but sometime in the spring which followed the diphtheria epidemic, I began to realize that Homer was growing up much faster than I was. Soon he would be a big brother like Cal or Charlie, not the same Homer I had gone to school with or helped explore the swamps in Florida. He was tall and gangling, and Mama was always letting out hems for him or lengthening suspenders. He was a very good shot. More and more, he wanted to hunt with the other boys. He did not quite know what to do with me.

One Sunday afternoon Homer suggested that we take a walk down by the river.

"Sure," I said. I had a feelin' about what was coming. When Papa or Mama wanted to have a private, heart-to-heart talk with one of us, they almost always took that one for a walk along the river, Papa especially.

The afternoon was warm and springy, just as if time had been imprisoned over the winter and was anxious to get out and exercise. Homer and I found violets blooming where we walked and birds of all kinds were busy building and repairing nests. A soft wind stirred the flowering branches, sending the petals cascading with a touch of perfume.

Homer and I sat down on the sloping embankment above one of the many pools on the river. We were silent for a long time, tossing pieces of wood into the stream and skipping flat stones. Finally, my brother said, "I gotta grow up. Understand?"

"I know," I said.

Homer found his words quickly now, as though it was only the beginning that had been hard for him. "The boys I can go with now don't want a little girl along. You gotta find you a friend. A girl, I think. Yeah, a girl."

I could not think of anyone right off. I knew lots of girls but none who liked to do the kind of things Homer and I had always done together. Apparently, he did not have anyone particular in mend either.

"I'll look out for you," he continued hurriedly. "Nobody's gonna hurt you while I'm around. If you want anything or need anything, you let me know. I'll get it."

I nodded. <u>Anything but me</u> hung in the air unspoken.

"Well," finished Homer. "I guess we better be getting back. It's getting late."

He took my hand and pulled me up the bank. The afternoon had a different feel to it on the way home, and the breeze was a little cooler, perhaps because the sun was going down.

From that day on, Homer was my big brother. I respected his wishes and stayed in the background when his new friends visited him at our house. I knew all about their pranks and escapades, fireworks make from black powder and the half-starved cats put in a neighbor's mailbox, but it was all second hand. I was no longer a participant.

Homer went to work at Papa's sawmill, and it became the part of his new life where I was the most welcome. I knew how to keep out of the way of the mill hands and could even make myself useful. Together, Homer and I carried out sawdust and cleaned the fire pits in the kiln drier and did many other jobs around the mill. It was hard work. I would come home almost too tired to eat and sleep, but I was happy to have spent the day with Homer. I was proud of him, too. I overheard the mill hands complimenting Papa on what a hard-working son he had.

In spite of the changes in our closeness, Homer and I still told each other everything, so I was the first to learn that he had a girl he was sweet on. Her name was Katherine, and he was miserable about the whole situation. He had nothing to wear but knickers and was ashamed to go courting in them, for they did not make him look very grown up. He wanted a long pants suit. I promised to help him persuade Papa it was needed.

At breakfast one morning, Homer glanced around the table, looked hard at me to indicate that the time had come and began his request in a quivery voice. "Papa, I need to get me some new clothes."

"He really does, Papa, I assured, nodding emphatically. "His pants are too small."

"I can lower the suspenders," Mama stated flatly.

Ordinarily, that would have been the end of it, but Homer and I had agreed to argue this time. I knew we had to make a strong case quickly, or the idea would drop.

"But, Papa," I persisted. "Homer's working hard at the mill and saving his money. He has a sweetheart, and he needs some long pants."

Homer boldly seconded the appeal, adding an argument of his own. "If'n I can't get me a suit working at the mill, Papa, Mr. Emrich will hire me at the Tall Pine Mill in town 'cause I'm 'sperienced."

"Well, I never!" said Mama. She was shocked and mad clear through at hearing backtalk, but Papa merely nodded.

"I've been thinking on it, son," he said, "even before you asked. You've been doing a man's work. Seems like you ought to have a man's privileges. Your mother can go with you and find you a suitable outfit. Emma, take the boy to town, and let him pick out a suit and what goes with it."

Mama had nothing it say to this, but everybody else began talking at once, all wanting new clothes. Papa turned his head to look each one in the face and stated, "The boy has earned it. He works hard, harder than some of the men, and I need him at the mill. Until I see the rest of you work like that, there'll be no more said about clothes."

As if someone had placed the lid on a bucket of chirping crickets, there was silence around the table. Everyone knew Papa meant what he said. I uncrossed my fingers and reached over to give Homer a friendly pinch. I wanted him to know how happy I was for him.

Mama decided to go to town early, and since she liked to drive the new horse, we took the buggy. I say "we" because Homer insisted that I go. Mama did not welcome the idea, but it was Homer's great day, so she finally gave in and let him manage it the way he liked.

We went to Hughes Department Store, the largest in town. The clerk looked all three of us over from head to foot. From his expression, he decided we were not wealthy enough to qualify as preferred customers, but he asked if he could be of help.

"Yes," said Mama rather sharply. The clerk's expression had not been lost on her either. "We want a long pants suit for this young man, and nothing shoddy."

"Yes, ma'am," smirked the salesman.

He went to the counter and began displaying a number of shop-worn things he had obviously failed to sell to other customers. He failed again. While Mama was examining these offerings and turning them down, one by one. I went over to a glassed-in closet where suits of better quality were kept. One was a beautiful dark greenish tweed. Without saying anything to Mama, I pulled the clerk's sleeves.

"Let Homer try on that 'un," I said.

The clerk looked down and brushed his sleeve. "Go away, brat," he said under his breath.

Knowing there were other ways to accomplish what I wanted, I motioned to Homer, and he came over. When I showed him the suit I had picked out, he liked it also. "Let me try on one like it in my size," he said.

"What size is that?" asked the clerk, looking sideways at the too-tight knickers Homer was wearing.

"You could measure him," I suggested pertly.

The clerk only glared at me, but Mama came to the rescue at that point. "Oh, son," she said in her flirty voice. "Has the nice man found one you like?"

Realizing that he might actually be on the way to selling an expensive garment, the clerk changed his approach. "One of our best worsted, ma'am," he fawned. "A bit - - a tiny bit - - more costly than some, but you won't find better quality." He smiled and took out his tape measure.

Homer's work at the mill had broadened his shoulders, and he was tall for his age. The clerk had no trouble finding one of the green tweed suits that would fit.

I tugged on Mama's skirt. "He needs a shirt and tie, too," I reminded, concerned that those articles might suffer for the expense of the new suit.

"Yes, of course," said Mama with a smile.

While the clerk located a white shirt in the same size as the suit, Homer selected a tie, a little lighter green than the suit and with a faint whirly streak of pale yellow. There were new shoes and socks to go with the rest, and a soft billed cap which matched the suit. When it was all chosen, Homer disappeared with the clerk into a dressing room, and Mama and I strolled around looking at all the new clothes.

We stopped beside a department store dummy which displayed a new fall outfit that Mama thought would look very becoming on her. She was taking off the pattern, so she could make one like it at home, when a handsome stranger came up behind her and put his arms around her. "How do you like it, ma'am?" he said.

Mama's hand came up to slap him before she realized who it was. When she recognized the stranger was Homer, she just stood for a moment open-mouthed. "Oh," was all she said.

I did not even have that much to say. Homer was certainly handsome in his new tweed suit, but he did not really look like my brother any more. He was slipping farther and farther away from me, and there was nothing I could do to stop it. I backed up to a rack of coats and wiped off some tears on the sleeve of one of them.

The clerk came up at that point. He complimented Homer on his appearance and asked if he would wear the suit.

That possibility brought Mama back her self-possession. "No. Ah- - no," she said. "That's a Sunday outfit. Wrap it, please, and we'll take it with us. How much is it?"

While Homer went to change back into his everyday clothes, the salesman began figuring the total price on a piece of paper. I had already added up the bill in my head as Homer chose the various articles. "It's $68.50, mister," I said.

"Just a minute," snapped the clerk.

I kept telling him my computation, and he kept muttering at me, until Mama intervened. "That's enough, miss Smarty," she ordered. "Let the man do the job he's hired for."

Homer got back before the clerk finished his calculations. Finally, he put down his pencil. "Sixty-eight, fifty," he said and looked at me as if he had eaten worms.

Mama counted out the money. When the clerk had the suit wrapped in a box, she picked it up, and we left the store. As we climbed into the buggy, she handed the reins to Homer. "I'm glad one of you is grown up," she said, looking sideways at me and clicking her tongue in disapproval of how I had made the clerk squirm. Then, a laugh got the better of her. "You sure brought him down a peg though," she acknowledged.

On the way home I dept looking over the seat of the buggy at Homer, reassuring myself that he was still the same person he had always been. I had an uneasy feeling, however, that the new suit marked an end or else a beginning. He seemed to sit a little straighter in the driver's seat and hold the reins with a little more authority.

The following Sunday morning our family was assembled in the front yard ready to go to church, all but Homer. I knew he was ready, too, for I had helped him knot the new green tie, just so, I wondered where he was, but I was sure he would be along in a minute. He never did anything without telling me about it, so if he had not been going to church with the rest of us, I would have known.

"Where is that slowpoke son of yours?" asked Mama, as Papa opened the gate.

"He'll be along, Emma," Papa replied with a twinkle in his eye. "Get in the car."

Always a willing traveler where the car was concerned, Mama seated herself primly in the front. Papa walked around the car to the driver's side. The rest of us scrambled in any which way, finding places as best we could.

We had just gotten ourselves arranged when the buggy passed us, freshly washed and shiny. Homer was driving all by himself. He beamed at us and waved and went on down the lane.

"Well, I never," said Mama. "And why can't he ride with the rest of this family?"

Papa chuckled. "The boy informed me that he was driving a lady friend to church this morning. I think you can understand his wanting to be alone, Emma. That is, if you can remember that far back."

"William!" said Mama in pretended outrage, but I noticed a smile on her face, too, a kind of fainter reflection of Papa's laugh.

I looked up the lane. Homer was just turning into the main road, to the left, toward Katherine's house. The horse pricked up his ears and began to trot, as though hearing a command from my brother. Hidden suddenly by the trees and the bank, the buggy disappeared.

This time there was no coat sleeve within easy reach, the way there had been in Hughes Department Store. I dabbed at my eyes with the back of my hand.

The end

About the Author

Ressie Chrenshaw Gray Watts, author of three books, numerous short stories, articles, and poems, started writing in elementary school, when she was presented with a notebook. Her love for reading and writing was encouraged by her teachers, and she published her first story in the local newspaper. At the age of seventeen, she moved to Minnesota, to care for her sister's children. She married, and lived with her husband on the Minnesota swamp bogs, until wolves scared and drove them to move to town. Later, widowed, with four children, she waitressed, worked at the post office, and cooked for a tuberculosis sanitarium. Remarried, she became involved with her husband's work at the local newspaper, the Kelliher Independent. She began to write for the paper. And became a member of Minnesota Press Women. She began with an advice column, and eventually, her Out of the Past articles focused on local folks, and their tales of coming to Minnesota, homesteading and surviving in the 1900's , and, on her own recollections of Arkansas and Florida, the Model T, hearing Charles Lindberg speak, and 'how things used to be'. Her experiences turned to words, in the true venue of a storyteller. Later, she moved with her family to California. She became a professional member of the National Writers Club, Women, published in California Highway Patrol, California Farmer, and Mc Calls. At the age of 92, Ressie approached the editor of the local newspaper and offered excerpts from her articles, and from

Homer and Me. The column has drawn many letters of appreciation, and requests for copies of the book. Her other works include Cippy, the fictional story, of a young girl raised in the Florida everglades by her fugitive father, and Depression Cabbage, an historical narrative, stories of coming to Minnesota, and surviving the depression era.

Printed in the United States
91428LV00003B/278/A